TREASURES REVEALED IN GOD'S WORD: BRINGING HOPE

BILLY ARCAND

Treasures Revealed in God's Word: Bringing Hope

Trilogy Christian Publishers A Wholly Owned Subsidiary of Trinity Broadcasting Network

2442 Michelle Drive Tustin, CA 92780

Rights Department, 2442 Michelle Drive, Tustin, CA 92780.

Trilogy Christian Publishing/TBN and colophon are trademarks of Trinity Broadcasting Network.

For information about special discounts for bulk purchases, please contact Trilogy Christian Publishing.

Trilogy Disclaimer: The views and content expressed in this book are those of the author and may not necessarily reflect the views and doctrine of Trilogy Christian Publishing or the Trinity Broadcasting Network.

Manufactured in the United States of America

10 9 8 7 6 5 4 3 2 1

Library of Congress Cataloging-in-Publication Data is available.

B-ISBN: 978-1-63769-044-4

E-ISBN: 978-1-63769-045-1

INTRODUCTION

Hello, everyone! I want to thank you for taking an interest in reading my book, *Treasures Revealed in God's Word: Bringing Hope.* I would like to share with you so many of the wonderful treasures I found in the Word of God: the Bible. There are so many types of treasure hunting. Let me mention some and see if you can relate to any of these. Fishing on a beautiful lake at sunrise and hearing the water swish against the side of the boat as the Canadian geese fly by; or panning for gold in a beautiful brook with the clean cool water swishing between the rocks, and the sun shining down when you see in your pan a beautiful piece of gold; or metal detecting along the beach during low tide in the early morning as the sun comes up. How about going to a yard sale on a beautiful day, or shopping the day after Thanksgiving, looking for that great deal or at the end of a season when just about everything is 70 to 80 percent off.

How do you feel when you find something that's great? Something you treasure. Something that means a lot. Well! In my book, I know you will find some great treasures. Maybe there will be some treasures nobody ever told you about or shared with you. Not only will I share these treasures with you, but I will also show you how you can keep these treasures. We all need in our life treasures of hope, love. peace, joy, contentment, relationships, friends, family, God, wisdom, discernment, understanding who we are, what our purpose is in our life, and much more. Speaking of purpose, did you know that God made us and has a purpose for each and every one of us? Did you know that He even knew us before and while we were being formed? God wants to give us a hope and a future that is good. The Bible has so many treasures, you cannot count them all. Countless promises and blessings all throughout His Word.

I have been studying the Bible for over fifty years, and I want to share them with you. I will be writing on subjects you might already understand, and there may be some things nobody has ever told you. I will also write on some things many of us were taught that are not in the Bible, but we are told it is in the Bible. I will also show you some things in the Bible that were kept secret for a religion's benefit instead of yours.

I hope and pray that my book will bring you all these treasures I mentioned and will bless you beyond measure. I will expound on these and set them in chapters to make it easy to separate one treasure from another. Before I begin, I have some questions many people ask when they're searching for meaning in life. I'm sure these will be questions you have heard and wondered, *What is the answer?* Every child is loaded with questions, and, as they grow older, there are even more. There's no age limit to having questions. Why, where, when, how. You took on more and more challenges as you grew older. Questions that come to every one of us, such as these thirty-nine questions I selected to answer in my book.

1. Who are we?
2. Where are we heading in life?
3. What will we be doing 10 years from now if the Lord wills?
4. Will I marry someone?

5. In the next generation, where will our country be?
6. Is there a God? Who is He?
7. What makes things grow from a little seed put in the ground
8. Why did Jesus speak in parables?
9. What is your opinion on the theory of evolution?
10. Do we really have a soul?
11. Is there an eternity after we leave this earth?
12. Is there life after death?
13. Why do some people live a real long life while others don't?
14. Why are there so many different religions? Which one is right?
15. Why are Christians persecuted and killed more than any other Religion?
16. Is there really a spiritual world? If so, is there really a battle going on for my soul? Your soul? America and the World?
17. If I hold onto unforgiveness towards someone who hurt me, will God really not answer my prayers?
18. Should we pray to Saints who have gone on before us?
19. Who are the Saints?
20. Are there Saints living here on earth now?
21. Why do some Religions say that Saints are only in Heaven?
22. Is Heaven and a Hell real?
23. Is Limbo real? If not, if not, why do some Religions teach this?
24. Is Purgatory real? If not, why do some religions teach on this?
25. Should we pray for people who have already passed on? Why do religions teach us that we should?

26. Why should we love and pray for our enemies? What good would that do for me?
27. I heard that there are different types of love. What are they?
28. Are their Angels here on earth?
29. What is the meaning of church to you? Is it the building you go to, or is it the people?
30. Why are their people who say they are Born Again? What does Born Again mean?
31. People tell me they are Saved. What does Saved mean?
32. Is it necessary for a Christian to have a career in politics? Is voting considered too worldly for Christians?
33. Is it necessary to go to church on a regular basis?
34. Is it necessary to go to church?
35. How do I hear from God?
36. What is a Baby Christian?
37. Why do some people think it's foolish to be a Christian, or think Christians are boring?
38. How can I know that God really loves me?
39. Why do I {Billy Arcand} want to share all this with you?

These are some questions we all have throughout our lifetime, from the springtime of a child all the way to the winter season of our senior years.

ABOUT THE AUTHOR

Hello! I'm Billy Arcand, author of *The Recurring Dream*, which was my first book, and now my second book: *Treasures of God's Word Revealed*. Before I start, I would like to share a little about myself.

I was born September the 17th, 1948 in Lawrence, Massachusetts, a city that had everything. I have great memories of growing up in my younger years. A very lively city with everything you could possibly think of was there. Always something to do, something to join, sports, a club. There were plenty of jobs even for kids, such as being a paper boy, shoveling snow for the elderly on your paper route, a lemonade stand, mowing grass, and more. As you got older, there were thousands of jobs available in the many stores and factories. There were big, beautiful movie theaters people from all over went to. Pool rooms, bowling allies, beautiful parks with trees and swimming pools, and everything you can think of for kids. There were activities like horseshoes, tennis, basketball, baseball, and ice skating and sledding in the winter. The outings were lots of fun with all the contests and free food, and I can't leave out all the beautiful band concerts playing so many beautiful patriotic and military songs every Sunday evening. So, yes! Lawrence had it all in those good old days. Lawrence was even in our old history books in all the schools back then for having so many factories, and they were some of the biggest in the world at that time.

In my teenage years, I took guitar lessons along with my brother Richard. We did everything together for many years in our childhood and teenage years. We formed a band called Hear They Are and played in many places for about four years. I can still remember to this day thinking to myself as I was on stage looking out to the audience as I was playing my bass guitar, *There's got to be more than this. Why do I feel like something is missing?* I know why now, which I found out why in February of 1970. I didn't have God in my life. This may sound foolish to some people, but God explains it in His Word, the Bible. You see! We were created by God, and we were created to know God and have Him in our lives. Without God, there's a void, and we spend our whole life trying to fill that void with many things that only bring a temporary, false fulfillment.

Have you ever seen people that just seem to be happy no matter what happens in their life? I remember seeing this before I became a Christian. Some Christians just had a glow and a peace about them that was hard to explain. What happens when you are in a dark place and suddenly you see a light? Immediately you look towards it. Well, that's what I saw in people that were living for the Lord before I became a Christian. I believe we all see this with our spiritual eyes. This may sound foolish to you, but we all live in a spiritual world just as much as a physical world.

Have you ever heard people say, "The battle is in the mind?" You see, we're all influenced by something, whether it be by the forces of good or evil. I can write a book on this subject alone but not now. It will take up too much of your time.

Let me briefly say this though: we all know deep down in our hearts that we long for the truth. Jesus said, "I am truth" (John 14:6). We all want to know and do the right thing.

What is the right thing? In my book I will give you answers to the best of my ability and will use the Bible to answer all of these questions. I will also quote statements from someone who went on record as being one of the wisest and richest men who ever lived. That was King Solomon, who wrote many proverbs that are still read today by people all over the world. That is the book of Proverbs in the Bible. He was King of Israel around 967 BC. He is also known for his downfalls in his life and turning to God in repentance and realizing life is empty without God in his life. He came to the conclusion that sin will separate us from fellowship with God. Throughout my book, I may quote some of his proverbs so that we can learn from his mistakes he made even though he was very wise and very rich. I will also use some of King David's quotes. God even said that he was a man after my own (God's) heart. I will also use quotes from Paul the Apostle who was a great Bible scholar at the time of Christ.

I believe you will enjoy reading all my answers, knowing that they will line up with the Word of God, the Bible. I believe these answers will open spiritual eyes, heal broken hearts, soften hearts that may be hard against God or people. I pray that you will find answers to these questions. You may even find some of these answers very liberating, releasing you from something that could have been oppressing you all your life. God loves you and so do I. His thoughts of you are always good. When you were born, He said it was good. You are His creation and His Love for you is unconditional. He loves you just the way you are and says, "Come unto me, all ye that labour and are heavy laden, and I will give you rest. Take my yoke upon you, and learn of me; for I am meek and lowly in heart: and ye shall find rest unto your souls. For my yoke is easy, and my burden is light" (Matthew 11:28-30).

CONTENTS

Chapter 1 1

Chapter 2 3

Chapter 3 5

Chapter 4 7

Chapter 5 11

Chapter 6 13

Chapter 7 17

Chapter 8 21

Chapter 9 23

Chapter 10 25

Chapter 11 29

Chapter 12 33

Chapter 13 35

Chapter 14 37

Chapter 15 41

Chapter 16 43

Chapter 17 47

Chapter 18 51

Chapter 19 55

Chapter 20 59

Chapter 21 61

Chapter 22 65

Chapter 23 69

Chapter 24 71

Chapter 25 73

Chapter 26 75

Chapter 27 79

Chapter 28 81

Chapter 29 85

Chapter 30 87

Chapter 31 91

Chapter 32 95

Chapter 33 99

Chapter 34 101

Chapter 35 105

Chapter 36 109

Chapter 37 113

Chapter 38 117

Chapter 39 125

CHAPTER 1
WHO ARE WE?

Genesis 1:26-27 says, "And God said, Let us make man in our image, after our likeness: and let them have dominion over the fish of the sea, and over the fowl of the air, and over the cattle, and over all the earth, and over every creeping thing that creepeth upon the earth; so God created man in his own image, in the image of God created he him; male and female created he them."

If you read from the beginning of Genesis, you will see that God created everything before creating man. To me, this shows a lot of love God has for us, knowing God prepared everything before creating us.

Jeremiah 29:11-12 says, "For I know the thoughts that I think toward you, saith the LORD, thoughts of peace, and not of evil, to give you an expected end. Then shall ye call upon me, and ye shall go and pray unto me, and I will hearken unto you."

Getting back to the question, *Who are we?* One thing I know for sure is that we are very much loved by God for Him to create everything first, then all of it for us. He knows us so much that He even knows the number of hairs on our head. Matthew 10:29-31 says, "Are not two sparrows sold for a farthing? and one of them shall not fall to the ground without your Father. But the very hairs of your head are all numbered." He says

1

in His Word that He even knew us before we were born, and while we were being formed in our mother's womb. Psalms 139:13-18 talks about that:

> For thou hast possessed my reins: thou hast covered me in my mother's womb. I will praise thee; for I am fearfully and wonderfully made: marvelous are thy works; and that my soul knoweth right well. My substance was not hid from thee, when I was made in secret, and curiously wrought in the lowest parts of the earth. Thine eyes did see my substance, yet being unperfect; and in thy book all my members were written, which in continuance were fashioned, when as yet there was none of them. How precious also are thy thoughts unto me, O God! How great is the sum of them! If I should count them, they are more in number than the sand: when I awake, I am still with thee.

There are literally hundreds and hundreds of verses in the Bible that tell us who we are, so I will just say this: God's love for us is more than any one of us can imagine. John 3:16-17 says, "For God so loved the world, that he gave his only begotten Son, that whosoever believeth in him should not perish, but have everlasting life. For God sent not his Son into the world to condemn the world; but that the world through him might be saved." In other words, no matter who you are, you are important and loved by God. I can write a book on what God thinks of you, His love, His mercy, and on who you are to God. I have to be brief on answering these questions and thank you for understanding.

CHAPTER 2
WHERE ARE WE HEADING IN LIFE?

Wouldn't it be great to know exactly where you will be next year, five years, or ten years from now? But that's impossible.

The way I see it, there are only two paths in life. One path leads to life and peace, and the other to death and destruction. This not only pertains to here on earth but into eternity also. We can only be going in one direction.

Jesus said I came to give life and life more abundantly (John 10:10). We live not only in a physical world but also a spiritual world. We all have a choice to either live in lightness or darkness, life or death. We are all born in sin which brings darkness and death, but Jesus came to give us life. He calls us to Him and to be a light in a dark world.

Matthew 5:16 says, "Let your light so shine before men, that they may see your good works, and glorify your Father which is in heaven."

Matthew 11:28-30 also says, "Come unto me, all ye that labor and are heavy laden, and I will give you rest. Take my yoke upon you, and learn of me; for I am meek and lowly in heart: and ye shall find rest unto your souls. For my yoke is easy, and my burden is light."

So, wherever we are heading in life, Jesus wants to make life better for us. He knows us better than we know ourselves.

3

Let Jesus take the wheel, if you haven't, and He will calm the storms of life and walk with you, strengthening us along the way. Whether it be down in the valley or on the mountain top, life is just too hard to do it alone. With Jesus, we are safe. With God, all things are possible. I can overcome all evil through Christ, who gives me strength. If you don't know Jesus as your Lord and Savior, He is right there waiting to hear from you. Just ask Him into your heart and life. Ask Him to forgive all of your past sins because all of us were born into sin and need a Savior as the Bible tells us. Jesus has His loving arms open wide to come into your life and give you salvation, peace, love, joy, and a whole new life this world cannot give. If you did this, all the angels in Heaven rejoice over one person who comes to Jesus and makes a decision to follow Christ. The Bible tells us this in Luke 15:10, which says, "Likewise, I say unto you, there is joy in the presence of the angels of God over one sinner that repenteth." Simply put, all the angels rejoiced over you in Heaven when you came to the Lord. My book is not only for the new Christian but also for the mature Christian.

CHAPTER 3

WHAT WILL I BE DOING TEN YEARS FROM NOW, AND WHAT DOES THE FURTURE HOLD FOR ME?

Well! This seems to be a question we all ask ourselves, especially as we start getting older. I've heard people in their sixties say, "I don't know what I want to be when I grow up." We worry about our future, which is natural. Will I be able to live comfortably when I retire? What will the economy be like in the future? Will we still have our freedom? There are many questions we ask ourselves. Will my faith be stronger? Is God calling me into any ministry? Should I go to school to learn a trade or a business? Should I be putting money aside for the future? Should I stay in the job I have now? Is there a future in my job, or will I not prosper if I stay where I'm at now? These are some examples we all experience.

The Bible says there is safety in a multitude of counselors. In other words, don't just go by one person's advice. In the Book of Proverbs 11:14, it says, "Where no counsel is, the people fall: but in the multitude of counsellors there is safety." Let me also say this, though: there are many counsellors that don't believe in God or are not mature spiritually in their walk with God, so you really have to be careful from where you get counsel on anything that has to do with your future.

Good counsel comes from good people with a good reputation of living a Godly life. Someone who isn't a Christian could believe it's okay to live a lifestyle contrary to the teachings of God. He could be a professor, teacher, or psychologist, etc. Good counsel comes through people who know God and are a good example of Godly living. If you are struggling with not knowing what you want to be, pray. Ask others what they see in you, but be careful where you get your advice. If someone tells you God wants you to do this or that, and if God didn't call you to this or that, then you will be miserable and not like what you are doing. Proverbs 16:16 says, "How much better is it to get wisdom than gold! and to get understanding rather to be chosen than silver!"

Here are some other good scriptures:

- "The ear that heareth the reproof of life abideth among the wise" (Proverbs 15:31)
- "The simple believes every word; but the prudent looks well to their going" (Proverbs 14:15).

In other words, be careful with people's suggestions. Make sure they are mature spiritually. Many Christians make big mistakes by going to unbelievers for Godly council. "Hear counsel, and receive instruction, that thou mayest be wise in thy latter end. There are many devices in a man's heart; nevertheless the counsel of the Lord, that shall stand" (Proverbs 19:20-21).

CHAPTER 4
I WOULD LOVE TO BE MARRIED, BUT I'M AFRAID OF MARRYING THE WRONG PERSON.

The Bible has a lot to say on marriage. The first marriage was instituted by God in the Garden of Eden. Have you ever considered what Eden means? Well! In the Hebrew, the word Eden has several definitions. Here is a list of uses in Hebrew for this word, Eden: 1). Place of pleasure, 2). He loves, 3). Delight, 4). Spot, 5). Moment, 6). Presence, 7). Open Door, and 8). Delightful. When you put these together, it means the place on earth where the presence of God was an open door to Heaven, a Delightful Place. Why am I telling you all this? Because this is what marriage is originally meant to be by our Creator before the fall.

Genesis 2:7 says, "And the Lord God formed man of the dust of the ground, and breathed into his nostrils the breath of life; and man became a living soul." Then, after creating Adam, God saw that it was not good that man should be alone, so He created the woman. God put Adam to sleep and took a rib from Adam and created the woman and presented her to Adam. This was the first marriage. You can read the whole story in chapter 2 of Genesis. As we look at marriage today, we should see marriage as a reflection of Christ and the church. A good solid marriage will have God in the center of their relationship with each other. The Bible says a threefold chord cannot be easily broken. When God is in the center of a marriage, it's like a threefold chord which makes your marriage a whole lot stronger. The husband and the wife must agree on this together to have this threefold chord.

Try taking two strings and pull hard on them. It will break with some strength. Now try with three strings. It's extremely hard to break. Many Christians fall into the trap of marrying someone who isn't a Christian, thinking they will be able change that person. It never happens, and it will hinder their walk with God and may even hinder them from a calling God had on them. You can't mix oil and water. The best and happiest marriages are the ones that do things God's way. Anything else may bring temporary satisfaction but eventually bring frustration, unhappiness, loneliness, despair, guilt, regret, and a number of other things. If you are a Christian and the other is not, you are depriving yourself of being the man or woman God is calling you to be. There's so much to be said on this subject, but the time and space necessary could take up the rest of this book. Loneliness is a very hard thing to handle as God even said in Genesis 2:18: "And the Lord God said, It is not good that man should be alone; I will make him an help meet for him."

God knows that, and He will help you and comfort you and bring the right one along when the time is right. You might say, "How long do I have to wait? I've been waiting and praying for years!" Well, God could have had someone right in your church, but you may not be involved in serving at your church, so you end up not seeing that special person. Don't look for love in all the wrong places. You know what really is attractive to the opposite sex? It's seeing that person living for the Lord. Seeing someone serving in any form of ministry at church. Get involved in activities at your church. By doing this, it will keep your mind off of being lonely. That someone special could be there just at the right time and place. If not, you are doing something in ministry that always will bring joy because you will be helping someone one way or another. Most churches have many things to get into, like a choir, praise team, playing an instrument, cleaning up after functions, or helping with cooking. Whatever you do, God is pleased, and you get an opportunity to serve which brings great reward. If you are engaged, I recommend that you both take a marriage course in a good Bible believing Christian church. Many churches offer this. We have no problem taking a course in something like computer science or art or public speaking, but when it comes to the decision of who we are going to spend the rest of our lives and maybe have children with, we think we don't need a marriage course. Believe me, we all need a marriage course.

I hope this helped. There are many great books on Christian marriage. Ask your pastor or someone at your church. They will be glad to let you know which book will be great to read.

CHAPTER 5
IN THE NEXT GENERATION, WHERE WILL OUR CHILDREN AND GRANDCHILDREN BE?

King Solomon, the wisest man on earth in his time said, "Train up a child in the way he should go: and when he is old, he will not depart from it" (Proverbs 22:6) This old but still powerful proverb had so much truth for so many centuries. I believe the reason why we don't see much progress in this proverb today is because many adults don't read the Bible. How can they teach their children what is right if they don't know themselves? There are way too many adults who are not living a Godly life; as a result, the children run wild. Let me give you some examples. Who is it that we see making terrible movies filled with violence and all manner of evil? It's the adults. Then we wonder why these kids today do such things. Who is passing laws making abortion legal? It's certainly not the kids. Who is teaching our children from kindergarten to college? It's the adults.

I don't have to get into too much detail. I'm sure most of us read enough stories on what these teachers teach our children. Things that do so much damage to the minds of these children. So where will our country be in the next generation? Dear, God! Please help us and save us! Only God knows. It's not good, that's for sure. We can see where many of these kids are politically because of what they were taught by these liberal teachers and professors. Many of them don't believe in God, so that alone should tell us where our country will be when these kids become adults and run our country. My prayer is that a revival sweeps across America, and not only gets ahold of these kids but also the teachers and professors. When a person becomes a Christian, their whole way of thinking changes for the good. They do the things that are right in God's eyes. This is also called a spiritual awakening. There always seems to be hardships just before a great move of God. Miracles happen through prayer. Keep praying for your children and grandchildren. Some day they will thank you for not giving up on them. If we don't pray for them, who will? Some day they will be running our country. If you're one of those parents praying for your child, don't get discouraged. Don't give up on them. Put them in God's hands. Keep God's promises in your heart. Treasure God's Word. The promises are for you also.

> "Believe on the Lord Jesus Christ, and thou shalt be saved, and thy house" (Acts 16:31).

> "The effectual fervent prayer of a righteous man availeth much" (James 5:16). Keep your children every day in your prayers.

> "This is the confidence that we have in him, that, if we ask any thing according to his will, he heareth us" (1 John 5:14). God also said it's His will that we all be saved.

Jesus was the greatest example in praying for your children. Jesus prayed for us a lot. Read John chapter 17. You will love the prayer He prayed for us.

CHAPTER 6
IS GOD REAL? WHO IS HE?

It's hard to believe that some people say they don't believe in God. Actually, Paul the Apostle, who was under the teachings of our Lord Jesus Christ, tells us that God has given all of us a measure of faith. We can lie to others or even to ourselves, but deep down inside, we all know God is real. We see His love for us in all of His creation.

Here are just a few Psalms which speak of God and His Love for us.

> When I consider thy heavens, the work of thy fingers, the moon and the stars, which thou hast ordained; What is man, that thou art mindful of him? and the son of man, that thou hast visitest him? For thou hast made him a little lower than the angels, and hast crowned him with glory and honour. Thou madest him to have dominion over the works of thy hands; thou hast put all things under his feet: All sheep and oxen, yea, and the beasts of the field; The fowl of the air, and the fish of the sea, and whatsoever passeth through the paths of the sea. O LORD our Lord, how excellent is thy name in all the earth!
>
> Psalm 8:3-9

Psalm 19:1 says, "The heavens declare the glory of God; and the firmament sheweth his handywork."

I really enjoy reading all the Psalms. They teach me how to pray and have a real relationship with God. There are so many beautiful Psalms that can calm the storms of life, heal the heart that is broken, and encourage the discouraged. They help us to really hear from God in so many circumstances. I will say this: there are some people who really don't want to believe God exists, and they will go to extremes trying to prove that there is no God. I pity those people and hope that they search for truth instead of trying to deny the existence of God. God says in His Word if you seek Him, you will find Him (Jeremiah 29:13).

The Gospel of John is a great place to start reading if you want God to show Himself and prove to you that He is real. Let Jesus talk to you through His Word.

How can anyone say they don't believe?

Just take a look around and consider all the beauties of nature. The beautiful flowers, so many kinds and colors. The trees for shade, and so many kinds. All the things built out of so many kinds of wood. The sun for light, growing food, and a number of other purposes. The moon by night, which also sets the tides, holding the water from passing over its boundary. Water which sustains all life. The oceans, lakes, ponds, rivers, brooks. The abundance of fish in these waters. The mountains and valleys. The seasons. The beautiful blue sky. The big fluffy clouds. The sun rises and sunsets. The beautiful animals, too many to count. The air we breathe and so much more. How can anyone not believe? I would bet there's not one farmer that doesn't believe in God. They see the miracle of a seed grow food after it's watered. They depend on God to send them rain. The Bible also is a great source of proving the existence of God. There are hundreds of prophecies of Christ that were written hundreds of years—even thousands of years—before Christ that give complete accuracy of the coming Christ who was to save the world from sin when we were gone astray.

Here is a list of just a few prophecies of Christ you could read that were written way before Christ:

- Isaiah 52:13-15
- Isaiah 53 - The whole chapter
- Psalms 22 - The whole chapter
- Psalms 16: 7-11
- Isaiah 7: 14
- Zechariah 9:9
- Zechariah 11:12-13
- Zechariah 12:10
- Daniel 7:13-14

These are just a few prophecies of Christ. These are proof that God is real; there's not just a few prophecies. There are hundreds all throughout the Old Testament. The Bible says, "Search the scriptures; for in them ye think you have eternal life: and they are they which testify of me" (John 5:39).

CHAPTER 7
WHAT MAKES THINGS GROW FROM A LITTLE SEED PUT IN THE GROUND?

Well! Let me start by quoting what the Bible says about each seed we see in all of our fruits and vegetables and all living creatures, both male and female.

> And God said, Let the earth bring forth grass, the herb yielding seed, and the fruit tree yielding fruit after its kind, whose seed is in itself upon the earth: and it was so. And the earth brought forth grass, and herb yielding seed after his kind, and the tree yielding fruit whose seed was in itself after his kind: and God saw that is was good.
>
> Genesis 1:11-12

Now let's look at all animal life. In verse 20, it says,

> And God said, Let the waters bring forth abundantly the moving creature that hath life, and fowl that may fly above the earth in the open firmament of heaven. And God created great whales, and every living creature that moveth, which the waters brought forth abundantly, after their kind, and every winged fowl after his kind: and God saw that it was good. And God blessed them saying, Be fruitful, and multiply, and fill the waters in the seas, and let fowl multiply in the earth. And the evening and the morning were the fifth day. And God said, Let the earth bring forth the living creature after his kind, cattle, and creeping thing, and beast of the earth after

his kind: and it was so. And God made the beast of the earth after his kind, and cattle after their kind, and every thing that creepeth upon the earth after his kind: and God saw that it was good.

Genesis 1:20-25

Did you notice how many times God mentioned "after its kind"? In other words—we never saw a pumpkin grow on an apple tree, or a dog having a baby sparrow. How about seeing a tomato seed! It will grow tomatoes. Did you ever notice how many seeds are in just one green bell pepper? Or how about a peach? There's only one seed in the peach and many in the bell pepper because that one seed can produce a whole tree full of peaches year after year, but the bell pepper is only one little plant, so God had it all figured out mathematically to keep everything in balance all throughout time. I love dissecting the scriptures. There are so many treasures in the Word of God.

So, getting back to the question! What makes a seed grow, and how? God makes it all happen. It's all God made gifts to us. We will know on the other side, when we meet God face to face. Then the story goes on to say that after God created all this, then He created us, man and woman, and said be fruitful and multiply and replenish the earth. In His great love, He created it all before creating man and said it was good.

Notice also how God said many times throughout Genesis chapter 1, "…and the evening and the morning were the first day." Then He said and the evening and the morning were the second day, all the way up to the seventh day. Well, as far as I know today has an evening and a morning within twenty-four hours, and you can go back all the way to the beginning and see there were always twenty-four hours in a day. I say this because there are people who try to say that, back then, it could have been many years and not days.

I hope these answers are giving you a better and deeper understanding of these questions. There's no such thing as a stupid question when it comes to asking any question that you might have concerning God and the Bible.

CHAPTER 8
WHY DID JESUS SPEAK IN PARABLES?

The use of parables by Jesus was a teaching method He used that fit into the tradition of His time. The parables of Jesus have been taught even until this day. There are stories from everyday living that convey messages. Many Bible scholars have commented that, although these parables seem simple, the messages they convey are deep and have spiritual meaning, also with a purpose for our benefit. The parables of Jesus remain some of the best stories in the world. Here are some of the parables Jesus spoke:

- "The Parables of the Sower" - Matthew 13:3-9
- "The Growing Seed" - Mark 4:26-29
- "The Two Debtors" - Matthew 18:23-35
- "The Lamp under a Bushel" - Matthew 5:14-15
- "Parable of the Good Samaritan" - Luke 10:25-37
- "The Friend at Night" - Luke 11:5-8
- "The Rich Fool" - Luke 12:16-21
- "The Wise and Foolish Builders" - Luke 6:46-49
- "New wine into Old Wineskins" - Luke 5:37-39
- "The Barren Fig Tree" - Luke 13:6-9
- "The Mustard Seed" - Matthew 13:31-32
- "The Leaven" - Luke 13:20-21
- "The Parable of The Pearl" - Matthew 13:45-46

- "Drawing in The Net" - Matthew 13:47-50
- "The Hidden Treasure" - Matthew 13:44
- "Counting the Cost" - Luke 14:28-33
- "The Lost Sheep" - Luke 15:4-6
- "The Unforgiving Servant" - Matthew 18:23-35
- "The Lost coin" - Luke 15:8-9
- "The Parable of the Lost Son" - Luke 15:11-32
- "The Unjust Steward" - Luke16:1-13
- "The Rich Man and Lazarus" - Luke 16:19-31
- "The Master and Servant" - Luke 17:7-10
- "The Unjust Judge" - Luke 18:1-8
- "Pharisees and the Publicans" - Luke 18:9-14
- "Workers in the Vineyard" - Matthew 20:1-6
- "The Two Sons" - Matthew 21:28-32
- "The Wicked Husbandmen" - Mark 12:1-9
- "The Great Banquet" - Matthew 22:1-14
- "The Budding of the Fig Tree" - Mark 13:28-31
- "The Faithful Servant" - Mark 13:34-37
- "The Ten Virgins" - Matthew 25:1-13
- "The Talents" - Matthew 25:14-30
- "The Sheep and the Goats" - Luke 14:7-14
- "The Parable of the Wedding Feast" - Luke 14-7-14

So, here we have some of the parables Jesus spoke two thousand years ago and are still great lessons for us today.

CHAPTER 9
WHAT IS YOUR OPINION ON THE THEORY OF EVOLUTION?

We were taught all throughout our school years the theory of evolution, which really brought on so much confusion. If you read the first chapter of Genesis, you will see how everything was created by God. As you read this, notice how God wants us to really understand that everything God created had its own seed which produced its own kind every time and nothing came through evolution. God spoke everything into existence. Notice what verse 11 says! "And God said, Let the earth bring forth grass, the herb yielding seed, and the fruit tree yielding fruit after his kind, whose seed is in itself, upon the earth: and it was so." Now, if you keep on reading; you will notice that God *many times* says "after his kind" for everything.

God created all the animals and everything that creeps on the earth *after his kind*. This abolishes the theory of evolution, and God wanted us to really get it by repeating over and over after his kind whose seed was in itself. God knows the future and saw people teaching the theory of evolution. There are many verses throughout the Bible where things have to be repeated over and over to make sure we get it.

Satan, the enemy of our soul, will try anything to deceive you into believing a lie. He works full time distracting people from the Truth. He will use people, news media, movies, books, teachers, professors, and even some preachers and pastors. Did I say preachers and pastors? Yup!

Jesus even talked about wolves in sheep's clothing.

Notice how God said many times after each thing He created "and it was so." I like that. In other words, what God says, goes. No if, ands, or buts about it.

I hope this cleared up any thoughts you might wonder concerning the theory of evolution. Satan would have you to believe in evolution to take your faith in God away from you. Like the Bible says, he is out to kill, steal, and destroy. Don't believe the lies of the enemy of your soul. Believe the Word of God. It's the Bread of Life. Jesus said, "It is written, Man shall not live by bread alone, but by every word that proceedeth out of the mouth of God" (Matthew 4:4).

CHAPTER 10
DO WE REALLY HAVE A SOUL?

To many people, this remains a mystery. The Bible has a lot to say about the soul. God created us with a soul which will spend eternity somewhere after this body of ours dies. If you look up the word soul in the Webster's dictionary, it says, "The spiritual part of a person that is believed to give life to the body, and in many religions is believed to live forever." Our body houses our soul. Our body is temporary, but our soul is eternal. A simple way to explain soul is our mind, will, and our emotions. Here are some scriptures taken from the Bible relating to the soul.

- "My soul shall make her boast in the Lord: the humble shall hear thereof, and be glad" (Psalms 34:2).
- "And the Lord God formed man of the dust of the ground, and breathed into his nostrils the breath of life; and man became a living soul" (Genesis 2:7).
- "And thou shalt love the Lord thy God with all thine heart, and with all thy soul, and with all thy might" (Deuteronomy 6:5).
- "And he stretched himself upon the child three times, and cried unto the Lord and said, O Lord my God, I pray thee, let this child's soul come into

him again. And the Lord heard the voice of Elijah; and the soul of the child came into him again, and he revived" (1 Kings 17:21-22).

- Then they cry unto the Lord in their trouble, and He brings them out of their distresses" (Psalms 107:28).

- "Return unto thy rest, O my soul; for the Lord hath dealt bountifully with thee. For thou hast delivered my soul from death, mine eyes from tears, and my feet from falling" (Psalms 116:7-8).

- The Lord redeemeth the soul of his servants: and none of them that trust in him shall be desolate" (Psalms 34:22).

- "My soul shall be joyful in the Lord: it shall rejoice in his salvation" (Psalms 35:9).

- "Why are you cast down, O my soul? And why art thou disquieted in me? hope thou in God: for I shall yet praise him for the help of his countenance" (Psalms 42:5).

- "Come and hear, all ye that fear God, and I will declare what he hath done for my soul" (Psalms 66:16).

- "For he commandeth, and raiseth the stormy wind, which lifteth up the waves thereof. They mount up to the heaven, they go down again to the depths: their soul is melted because of trouble" (Psalms 107:25-26).

- And fear not them which kill the body, but are not able to kill the soul: but rather fear him which is able to destroy both soul and body in hell" (Matthew 10:28).

- "For what is a man profited, if he shall gain the whole world, and lose his own soul? or what shall a man give in exchange for his soul?" (Matthew 16:26).

- "Then saith he [Jesus] unto them, My soul is exceeding sorrowful, even unto death: tarry ye here, and watch with me" (Matthew 26:38).

- "And I will say to my soul, Soul, thou hast much goods laid up for many years; take thine ease, eat, drink, and be merry. But God unto him, Thou fool, this night thy soul shall be required of thee: then whose shall those things be, which thou hast provided? So is he that layeth up treasure for himself, and is not rich toward God" (Luke 12:19-21).

- "And when they had preached the gospel to that city, and had taught many, they returned again to Lystra, and to Iconium, and Antioch, confirming the souls of the disciples, and exhorting them to continue in the faith, and that we must through much tribulation enter into the kingdom of God" (Acts 14:21-22).

So, there we have it. I hope these scriptures gave you a good understanding. Actually, I know these scriptures did give you a better understanding of our soul.

CHAPTER 11
IS THERE AN ETERNITY AFTER WE LEAVE THIS LIFE?

This is a question everyone ponders one time or another. You are not alone on this. We all wonder where we will go if there is something beyond what we are living here and now! The scriptures I mentioned about the soul would fit nicely with this question; however, I will show you some verses that will also help you to understand eternity.

- "For thus saith the high and lofty One that inhabiteth eternity, whose name is Holy; I dwell in the high and holy place with him also that is of a contrite and humble spirit, to revive the spirit of the humble, and to revive the heart of the contrite ones" (Isaiah 57:15).
- "The eternal God is thy refuge, and underneath are the everlasting arms: and he shall thrust out the enemy from before thee; and shall say, Destroy them" (Deuteronomy 33:27).
- "And, behold, one came and said unto him, Good Master, what good thing shall I do, that I may have eternal life?" (Matthew 19:16).
- "That whosoever believeth in him should not perish, but have eternal life. For God so loved the

world, that he gave his only begotten Son, that whosoever believeth in him should not perish, but have everlasting life" (John 3:15-16).

- "These words spake Jesus, and lifted up his eyes to heaven, and said, Father, the hour is come; glorify thy Son, that thy Son also may glorify thee: As thou hast given him power over all flesh, that he should give eternal life to as many as thou hast given him. And this is life eternal, that they might know thee the only true God, and Jesus Christ, whom thou hast sent" (John 17:1-3).

- "Then Simon Peter answered him, Lord, to whom shall we go? thou hast the words of eternal life" (John 6:68).

- "And I give unto them eternal life; and they shall never perish, neither shall any man pluck them out of my hand" (John 10:28).

- "For the invisible things of him from the creation of the world are clearly seen, being understood by the things that are made, even his eternal power and Godhead; so that they are without excuse" (Romans 1:20).

- "While we look not at the things which are seen, but at the things which are not seen: for the things which are seen are temporal; but the things which are not seen are eternal" (2 Corinthians 4:18).

- "For we know that if our earthly house of this tabernacle were dissolved, we have a building of God, an house not made with hands, eternal in the heavens" (2 Corinthians 5:1).

- "And when the Gentiles heard this, they were glad, and glorified the word of the Lord: and as many as were ordained to eternal life believed" (Acts 13:48).
- "Now unto the King eternal, immortal, invisible, the only wise God, be honor and glory for ever and ever. Amen" (1 Timothy 1:17).

These are just a few I mentioned concerning eternity, but there are more all throughout the Bible.

.

CHAPTER 12
IS THERE LIFE AFTER DEATH?

There are many people who died and came back to life and claim they were sent back because God had more for them to do. Some people also claim they were heading for Hell, and God spared them, gave them another chance, and were sent back to this life.

The Apostle Paul taught us that there is life after death. "And as it is appointed unto man once to die, but after this, the judgment" (Hebrews 9:27). I would recommend reading the rest of the chapter. In doing this, the Apostle Paul explains that our salvation is not based on our own works, but on the blood sacrifice of our Lord Jesus Christ.

- "For the wages of sin is death; but the gift of God is eternal life through Jesus Christ our Lord" (Romans 6:23).
- "For God so loved the world, that he gave his only begotten Son, that whosoever believeth in Him should not perish, but have everlasting life" (John 3:16).
- "Verily, verily, I say unto you, He that heareth and believeth on him that sent me, hath everlasting life, and shall not come into condemnation; but is passed from death unto life" (John 5:24).

- "He that believeth on the Son hath everlasting life: and he that believeth not the Son shall not see life; but the wrath of God abideth on him" (John 3:36).
- "Then Peter said, Lo, we have left all, and followed thee. And he [Jesus] said unto them, Verily I say unto you, There is no man that has left house, or parents, or brethren, or wife, or children, for the kingdom of God's sake, who shall not receive manifold more in this present time, and in the world to come life everlasting" (Luke 18:28-30).

A little note on this verse: God is able to give us more than we can ever imagine when we put God first in our life. Like it says in the book of Matthew, "But seek ye first the kingdom of God and His righteousness, and all these things shall be added unto you" (Matthew 6:33).

Sometimes, or should I say many times, it's hard to seek the kingdom of God and His righteousness first. We live in a microwave society, and we want everything right away. We get impatient watching the pot, waiting for the water to boil. We put something in the microwave for three minutes and stare at the seconds go by, tapping our finger on the counter, thinking it's taking too long, so we end it after two and a half minutes. We text or send instant messages and get instant answers when people used to send letters in the mail and waited for weeks or even months for a reply. Waiting on God can be hard, but when God answers a prayer, nothing can be better. God knows us better than we know ourselves. Psalms 27:14 says, "Wait on the Lord. Be of good courage. Wait I say on the Lord and He shall strengthen thine heart."

I hope these scriptures helped you to understand that there really is life after death for us when we leave this earth.

CHAPTER 13
WHY DO SOME PEOPLE LIVE A LONG LIFE, WHILE SOME DON'T?

Well, I can't come up with my own answer or opinion. All I can do is give you some scriptures and hopefully give you a better understanding of the mysteries of God. The Bible does say in Romans, "O the depth of the riches both of the wisdom and knowledge of God: how unsearchable are His judgments, and His ways past finding out!" (Romans 11:33).

Actually, when God created man, we were made to live forever, but sin caused death. If you read the book of Genesis, you will see that after the fall, man's life got shorter and shorter as you read about the lives of different people. Each generation lived less years than the previous generation. The Bible says, "When it rains, it rains on the just and the unjust" (Matthew 5:45).

I've seen good people die young and evil people die young. I've also seen good people live a long life, and I've seen evil people live a long life. Who knows the mind of God? One thing I do know is that God loves us and is good. Maybe God looks into the future of someone and decides to take him or her home before this person got trapped into something really bad. We can think up all kinds of things, but we will know the real reason when we meet God, then it will all make sense.

CHAPTER 14
WHY ARE THERE SO MANY DIFFERENT RELIGIONS? WHICH ONE IS RIGHT?

Let me start out with why I think there are so many different religions before I tell you which one is right. Before man was created by God, and even before the earth was created by God, He created angels. According to scripture, Lucifer was one of those angels and was once a beautiful angel and was actually the most powerful angel that was placed in charge of all the music and praise and thanksgiving to God. He developed a seed of pride in himself and tried to exalt himself above God and take God's place in Heaven. If this sounds a little strange to you, you can read about this in the Bible, in the book of Isaiah.

> How art thou fallen from heaven, O Lucifer, son of the morning! how art thou cut down to the ground, which didst weaken the nations! For thou hast said in thine heart, I will ascend into heaven. I will exalt my throne above the stars of God: I will sit also upon the mount of the congregation, in the sides of the north: I will ascend above the heights of the clouds; I will be like the most High. Yet thou shalt be brought down to hell, to the sides of the pit. They that see thee shall narrowly look upon thee, and consider thee, saying, Is this the man that made the earth to tremble, that did shake the kingdoms; that made the world as a wilderness, and

destroyed the cities thereof; that opened not the house
of his prisoners?

Isaiah 14:12-17

Luke 10:18 says, "[This is Jesus talking to His disciples]
And He said unto them, I beheld Satan as lightning fall
from Heaven." Lucifer means "Morning Star." Satan means
"Adversary." Now! What does all this have to do with the
question, why are there so many different religions? Which
one is right?

Well! The reason I brought up these scriptures is to give you
a good understanding of the real reason why there are so many
religions all around the world. Satan doesn't want anyone wor-
shiping God, so he will set up any religion you wish, just for
you—as long as it's not the real religion. The Bible says Satan
is a liar and a deceiver. He will keep you from knowing God
through all these religions. In the Gospel of John, Jesus says,
"I am the way, the truth, and the life: no man cometh unto the
Father, but by me" (John 14:6).

Why do you think there are people who don't pray in
Jesus' name? Satan puts it in their head, and they fall for it.
To learn more on Jesus being the only way, the truth, and
the life, I recommend reading chapters 14 through 17 of the
gospel of John.

When Jesus was here on earth, you can read in the gospel
of Matthew how Satan even tried to get Jesus to bow down and
worship him.

> Again, the devil taketh him up into an exceeding high
> mountain, and sheweth him all the kingdoms of the
> world, and the glory of them; And saith unto him, All
> these things will I give thee, if thou wilt fall down and

worship me. Then saith Jesus unto him, Get thee hence, Satan: for it is written, Thou shalt worship the Lord thy God, and him only shalt thou serve.

(Matthew 4:8-10).

Notice the last five words? "Him only shalt thou serve." In other words, *no other god*. No other religion, period. God loves us and doesn't want us to be deceived into the lies of Satan, who is only out to kill, steal, and destroy. If you would like more information on this subject, I mentioned a lot on this in my other book *The Recurring Dream*, Jesus tells us not to worship other gods for our own good. He is the Good Shepherd of the sheep.

CHAPTER 15

WHY ARE CHRISTIANS PERSECUTED AND KILLED FOR THEIR FAITH MORE THAN ANY OTHER RELIGION?

There are many stories of Christian persecution we can read about throughout history since the time of Christ. We live in a spiritual world just as much as a physical world. We read about Satan in the previous chapters; how that he is out to kill, steal, and destroy. He will trick people into any religion you prefer, just as long as it's not the true, one, and only religion, which is following the teachings of Christ. You may ask, what does this have to do with the question? Well, people are either for or against God. Jesus said, either you are for Me or against Me. In other words, people are persuaded one way or another. There are many countries that forbid the teachings of Christ. The people that rule in these countries can easily be led by the powers of darkness because they allow Satan to rule over them and many don't even realize it. Jesus is the Great Shepherd, and we are the sheep. Jesus came to save us all from Satan's power when we were gone astray. Like the song goes, "O tidings of Comfort and Joy."

When we turn to God and become a Christ follower, the Bible says that all things become new in Christ. but it also says we will suffer persecution. That's why Jesus said you must be born again. "Jesus answered and said unto him, Verily, verily, I say unto thee, Except [or unless] a man be born again, he cannot see the kingdom of God" (John 3:3). This may sound foolish to the world, but, to us who believe, it's the power of God unto salvation.

The Bible tells us that the Word of God is foolishness to those who don't know God: "For the preaching of the cross is to them that perish foolishness; but unto us which are saved it is the power of God" (1 Corinthians 1:18).

It also says it's an offence to some people, so they let the devil, Satan, use them to come against Christians without even realizing it. Actually, there are some who do know what they are doing and refuse to associate themselves with Jesus and the Word of God, which I find to be very sad. Christian persecution is all over the world. Some more, some less. People are thrown into prison, and in some countries are killed. The people that do this to Christians are led by Satan, and some don't even realize it. If you haven't read my book *The Recurring Dream* yet, I go into a lot more detail on this subject. If you read the four Gospels and the book of Acts, you will see how there really is a spiritual war between good and evil for our soul. This is why Christians are so persecuted more than any other religion. Satan uses whoever he can to persecute Christians, but God is faithful and will always fight our battles for us as we look to Him. There are many scriptures all throughout the Bible that tell us of that spiritual battle. Jesus mentions this all throughout the four gospels. I hope this helped in understanding why Christians are killed and persecuted more than any other religion.

CHAPTER 16

IS THERE REALLY A SPIRITUAL WORLD? IF SO, IS THERE A BATTLE GOING ON FOR MY SOUL, AMERICA, AND THE WORLD?

Most of us know the story of Adam and Eve, how they listened to Satan and gave into his temptations to sin against God. This is where it all started here on the earth. Let me begin by saying there are both spirits of good and evil. For example, if you are saved, the Holy Spirit is right there with you, comforting you, leading you into the right ways. Jesus also called the Holy Spirit the Comforter. Here are some scriptures that go into more detail:

- "And I will pray the Father, and he shall give you another Comforter, that he may abide with you for ever; Even the Spirit of truth; whom the world cannot receive, because it seeth him not, neither knoweth him: but ye know him; for he dwelleth with you, and shall be in you" (John 14:16-17).
- "(For the weapons of our warfare are not carnal, but mighty through God to the pulling down of strongholds;) casting down imaginations, and every high thing that exalteth itself against the knowledge of God, and bringing into captivity

every thought to the obedience of Christ" (2 Corinthians 10:4-5).

- "For such are false apostles, deceitful workers, transforming themselves into the apostles of Christ. And no marvel; for Satan himself is transformed into an angel of light" (2 Corinthians 11:13-14).
- "For we wrestle not against flesh and blood, but against principalities, against powers, against the rulers of the darkness of this world, against spiritual wickedness in high places. Wherefore take unto you the whole armour of God, that ye may be able to withstand in the evil day, and having done all, to stand, Stand therefore, having your loins girt about with truth, and having on the breastplate of righteousness; And your feet shod with the preparation of the gospel of peace; Above all, taking the shield of faith, wherewith ye shall be able to quench all the fiery darts of the wicked" (Ephesians 6:12-16).

These scriptures here make it very clear that there is a spiritual world as Paul the Apostle taught throughout his epistles. Politics is definitely one of the areas where there's always a spiritual battle, especially during voting season.

- "No weapon that is formed against thee shall prosper; and every tongue that shall rise against thee in judgment thou shalt condemn. This is the heritage of the servants of the Lord, and their righteousness is of me, saith the Lord" (Isaiah 54:17).

- "Be sober, be vigilant; because your adversary the devil, as a roaring lion, walketh about, seeking whom he may devour" (1 Peter 5:8).

There are many more scriptures that refer to a spiritual world, and you will find them all throughout the Bible. I wrote a lot on this also in my other book *The Recurring Dream*, a Christian Fiction Novel. I hope this helped you to understand that there is a spiritual world as well as a physical world.

CHAPTER 17

IF I HOLD ONTO UNFORGIVENESS TOWARDS SOMEONE WHO HURT ME, WILL GOD REALLY NOT ANSWER MY PRAYERS? I WAS TOLD I MUST FORGIVE AND LET GO BUT IT'S HARD.

Let's see what God says in His Word.

This is part of the Lord's Prayer that Jesus was teaching:

- "And forgive us our debts as we forgive our debtors" (Matthew 6:12).
- "For if ye forgive men their trespasses, your heavenly Father will also forgive you: But if ye forgive not men their trespasses, neither will your Father forgive your trespasses" (Matthew 6:14-15).
- "Then came Peter unto him, and said, Lord, how oft shall my brother sin against me, and I forgive him? till seven times? Jesus saith unto him, I say not unto thee, Until seven times: but, Until seventy times seven" (Matthew 18:21-22).
- "So likewise shall my heavenly Father do also unto you, if ye from your hearts forgive not every one his brother their trespasses" (Matthew 18:35).

When someone has hurt or disappointed you, the logical response would be to think you're hurting them by not forgiving them and holding a grudge. The harsh truth is that you're actually causing yourself more pain by holding onto the anger, and the person that you wish not to forgive has the subconscious power to control you. However, you can get disconnected from the power of control when you forgive. Be aware of negative emotions that you feel towards the other person, including jealousy, anger, hatred, hurt, and bitterness. Awareness will help you to acknowledge the need to forgive. Holding onto these things are highly toxic and not good for your health, both physically and spiritually.

When you feel ready to forgive, make arrangements to get together with that person that has hurt you and express yourself. Talking things over helps you to let go and heal. Actually, it's medically proven that people who hold a grudge for long periods of time get ill with a disease. It's like a cancer that eats away your life. It is true that medical research shows us that unforgiveness causes health problems including cancer. According to much research by The Science Times and many others reported on web sites that 61 percent of cancer patients have unforgiveness issues. Suppressed anger- people that often get angry have issues associated with unforgiveness. Just google 61 percent of cancer patients have unforgiveness. You will see lots of reports on this.

Bitterness increases the risk of depression. When you forgive the person that did something or said something to you, you actually are releasing a bondage between you and that person. If we want to love, we must learn to forgive. You must remember that forgiveness is always for you. By doing this, you free yourself. The same goes with repenting to God and asking forgiveness for something you did against God. Remember, you can be your own worst critic, letting Satan come, accuse you, and bring up something you did five years ago when God has already forgiven you. In the Bible, there are many passages referring to God's forgiveness when we ask for it. Here are two I like a lot.

- 'As far as the east is from the west, so have I forgiven your transgressions" (Psalm 103:12).

The Bible says He drowns your sins in His sea of forgetfulness when we ask. "He will turn again, he will have compassion upon us; he will subdue our iniquities; and thou wilt cast all their sins into the depths of the sea" (Micah 7:19). There are many scriptures that talk of the forgiveness of God, and, when He forgives us, the accuser and the enemy of our soul will always try to bring up the past.

In other words, Jesus doesn't even remember them. Don't let things of the past keep haunting you and bringing you down. When God forgives you, don't hold onto condemnation. This kind of thinking can be spiritually destructive.

The battle is in the mind, and that's where the enemy of your soul does his battling. When he reminds you of something, just say, "I'm forgiven." Thank you, Jesus. That alone will send him far away. The devil trembles at the sound of that name Jesus: "And I heard a loud voice saying in heaven, Now is come salvation, and strength, and the kingdom of our God, and the power of his Christ: for the accuser of our brethren is cast down, which accused them before our God day and night" (Revelation 12:10).

I hope this helped you in the importance of forgiveness. There are many good books on unforgiveness and the power of forgiveness that brings healing both physically and spiritually.

CHAPTER 18
SHOULD WE PRAY TO SAINTS WHO HAVE GONE ON BEFORE US?

Before I answer this question, I would like to say that the answers I give are not my own. They are from the Holy Bible. What does the Holy Bible say about this? "Jesus said unto him, I am the way, the truth, and the life; no man comes unto the Father but through me" (John 14:6).

Okay, Let's break this down so we can really get a good understanding of what Jesus is saying here. By saying "I am," He wasn't talking about anyone else accept Him—not another man, woman, or religion. Not another pastor, priest, saint, or whoever comes to your mind. Nobody. So, now that we know that, let's read it again. Jesus said "I am the way, the truth, and the life, No man comes to the father but through me."

Now let's break down the way. "The way to what?" You may ask!

The way to the Father. In other words, the only way to get to God the Father is through Jesus—nobody else. Religion will tell you there are other ways, but Jesus said there is no other way. Jesus had to say this because He knew there would be many religions that would tell you something different. Satan is a liar and there's no truth in him. He is the one behind it all, deceiving people into praying to everyone except Jesus, the one who is our High Priest, our mediator between us, and God the Father.

Okay, next He said, "the truth." So, now we have the way and the truth. Everything else is a lie; it's like saying I am the way and it's the truth, and everything else is a lie. The opposite of the truth is something that is not the truth. This is why Jesus said, "I am the truth." Remember, Satan is the author of all lies and confusion. He will try to get people into believing anything, as long as you don't pray to the Father in Jesus' name. People will tell you there are many ways to God and ask, "What makes you think your religion is the only truth?" This is what Satan puts in the minds of people all over the world. It sounds good, but it's not the truth. Remember Jesus said when asked "What is truth?" He said *I am truth.* There is not one religion or person that fulfilled hundreds of prophecies hundreds and even thousands of years before Christ. Jesus made it plain and simple saying, "I am the way, the truth, and the life, No man comes to the Father but through me." Okay. The way, the truth, and the life.

Let's break it down, "the life." No other religion paid the penalty for our sins but Jesus. He did this the exact way that it was predicted hundreds of times in the Old Testament. No religion can give us eternal life except Jesus. So here we have it: "the way, the truth, and the life, No man can come to the Father but through me." So now you know and please don't let anyone try and tell you that you get to the heart of God through this person or that person. That's an insult to Jesus because it was Him that made the way for us to get to the Father. The world and Satan will confuse this subject, but Jesus made it plain and simple.

Now, after reading this, you know more about what the Bible says about not praying to any other god, saint, or angel. If you would like to learn more on this, read the four Gospels and the Epistles. There are many places in the Bible where people bowed and prayed to saints and angels, but they said, do not pray to me. Stand upon your feet for I also am a man. Worship God; He is your creator. He made you and Loves you. You have Eternal Life through Christ, not anyone else. He is the one who deserves the Praise (Acts 15).

In the religion I grew up in, I was given a patron saint to pray to at my confirmation. I was told that whenever I lose something to pray to Saint Anthony, and he would answer my prayer. Now we learned that Jesus is who we pray to, not a saint. Jesus is the mediator between God and man, nobody else. I hope this helped in understanding that God hears our prayers, and the enemy would have you praying to anyone, as long as it's not God.

CHAPTER 19
WHO ARE THE SAINTS?

In many of the Christian churches, the word saint is used more generally to refer to anyone who is a Christian. This is similar in usage to Paul's numerous references to the New Testament of the Bible. If this is the case, why do some churches teach that saints are only in Heaven? I will jot down some scriptures written by Paul the Apostle to help you to understand this very touchy subject. Let's remember now that Paul the Apostle was taught by Jesus Christ. When the Apostle Paul wrote letters to the churches, many times he used the word saints referring to the Christians of the churches he was writing to at that time. In other words, saint means sacred, holy, saved, redeemed, born again, or sanctified. This is a free gift to us from God when we accept Jesus into our heart as Lord and Savior. The Bible says, "Believe on the Lord Jesus Christ, and thou shalt be saved, and thy house" (Acts 16:31).

This is not done by our good deeds, but by simply accepting the free gift of Salvation Jesus provided for all those who turn to Him, invite Jesus to forgive their sin. It's that simple. The Bible says, "For by grace are ye saved through faith; and that not of yourselves: it is the gift of God: Not of works, lest any man should boast" (Ephesians 2:8-9).

Okay, getting back to scriptures on Saints.

- "Among whom are ye also called of Jesus Christ: to all that be in Rome, beloved of God, called to be saints: Grace to you and peace from God our Father, and the Lord Jesus Christ" (Romans 1:6-7).
- "Be kindly affectioned one to another with brotherly love; in honor preferring one another; Not slothful in business; fervent in spirit; serving the Lord; rejoicing in hope; patient in tribulation; continuing instant in prayer; distributing to the necessity of the saints; given to hospitality" (Romans 12:10-13).

Question! If saints are only in Heaven, like some religions tell us, then why did Paul the Apostle mention their needs? There's no need in Heaven. Needs are here on earth, not in Heaven. Here we are reading about giving to the saints that are in need in their church. Wow! If you were never told this, then this is one of the many treasures that are in the Bible for you to discover as you read God's Word, the Bible. "I commend unto you Phebe our sister, which is a servant of the church which is at Cenchrea: that ye receive her in the Lord, as becometh saints, and that ye assist her in whatsoever business she hath need of you: for she has been a succourer of many, and of myself also" (Romans 16:1-2).

Two things I want to mention in these verses. First, Phebe was called a saint and sister in the Lord. Second, sounds like Phebe was a great woman of God who gave and helped many people in the church in their times of difficulty and need.

"Unto the church of God which is at Corinth, to them that are sanctified in Christ Jesus, called to be saints, with all that in every place call upon the name of Jesus Christ our Lord, both their's and our's; Grace be unto you and peace from God our Father, and from our Lord Jesus Christ" (1 Corinthians 1:2-3).

This is how Paul the Apostle addressed the church when writing a letter to the Saints. What a contrast to what a lot of us were taught in religion class. "Dare any of you, having a matter against another, go to the law before the unjust and not before the saints?" (1 Corinthians 6:1). What Paul is saying here is, don't go to the unbeliever when you have a disagreement or quarrel, but go to someone in your church that is a trustworthy and spiritually mature Christian that can find a resolution to your problem.

- "For God is not the author of confusion, but of peace, as in all churches of the saints" (1 Corinthians 14:33).
- "Paul the Apostle of Jesus Christ by the will of God, to the saints which are in Ephesus and to the faithful in Christ Jesus" (Ephesians 1:1).

Paul was addressing them as saints and faithful in Christ Jesus. "And he gave some to be Apostles, and some Prophets, and some Evangelists, and some Pastors and Teachers; (for the perfecting of the Saints) and for the work of the Ministry, for the edifying of the body of Christ" (Ephesians 4:11-12).

Notice Paul saying for the perfecting of the saints. In other words, God raised up apostles, prophets, evangelists, pastors, and teachers to perfect the saints of these churches here on this earth while these Christians (saints) were growing in the Lord. They were ordinary people who gave their life to Christ and were under Paul's teachings, growing in the faith. This sounds very different than what many people are taught in his letter to the Ephesians.

In the eyes of God, the minute you turn to Christ and ask Him into your life, accept that free gift of Salvation Jesus offers to all of us, then in God's eyes, you are a saint made holy, sanctified, saved because of Christ, and what He did to pay for your sins and mine. "Salute every saint in Christ Jesus. The brethren which are with me greet you. All the saints salute you, chiefly they that are of Caesar's household" (Philippians 4:21-22).

Paul is saying here to acknowledge your brethren when you see them. Don't just walk by without being courteous. He is also saying all the saints of Caesar's household say hello. If the saints are saying hello, then they had to be here on earth. I'm sorry if I am stressing this a little too much, but I came from a background that prayed to saints, taught that saints are only in Heaven, and only the Pope could declare someone a saint after that person died.

In closing, I will just show you one more scripture which I feel is a good one to end with concerning Saints.

- "For God is not unrighteous to forget your work and labor of love; which you have showed toward his name; in that you have ministered to the saints and do minister" (Hebrews 6:10).

Okay, I believe you have a better understanding of Saint. I wanted to share this with you to clear up all the confusion.

CHAPTER 20
ARE THERE SAINTS LIVING HERE ON EARTH NOW?

Well, we just read about what the Apostle Paul wrote in his days; and it's the same today. Religion is manmade and has many flaws and misinterpretations. The Word of God doesn't change. There are many scriptures referring to God saying I am the same yesterday, today, and forever, I change not.

Although Christians are saints in God's eyes, individuals really would not want to be called saint so and so; just like in the days of Paul. He addressed the whole church as saints, but when writing to an individual, he used the term brother or sister in the Lord and that still applies today. If you read the Epistles, you will see that every time the Apostle Paul wrote a letter to different churches, he addressed them as saints.

We don't become a saint by any good deeds. Our works of righteousness could never meet up to God's standards. What makes us holy, sacred, virtues etc. is only by what Christ done for us in order to obtain salvation. Only when we come to Jesus and accept his free gift of salvation to all those who call on Him. "For the wages of sin is death, but the gift of God is eternal life through Jesus Christ our Lord" (Romans 6:23).
We don't earn salvation; it's given to us free. Thank God!

CHAPTER 21
WHY DO SOME RELIGIONS SAY THAT SAINTS ARE ONLY IN HEAVEN?

I just can't understand why they would teach such a thing when it's written so plainly in so many books in the Bible. The only conclusion I can come up with is (which I say, so many times throughout my books) we live in a spiritual world just as much as a physical world. Satan is the author of all lies and confusion. Many religions will glorify people who died and teach you to pray to them, making you believe that in doing so you can get prayers answered. This is a trick of Satan to sway you away from the truth; away from Jesus. This is why Jesus said in the Gospels, "I am the way, the truth, and the life, No man comes to the Father but through me."

Jesus is the one who is the mediator between God and man. Religion will tell you that a priest, a saint, or whoever else you can think of is the mediator and can get to the heart of God better than through Jesus, but this is not true and is what Satan would want you to believe. Just as long as you are not praying to God through Jesus, Satan will leave you alone and that's exactly how he would want it. Satan is a liar and has nothing to do with God and gets people to teach anything but the truth. One drop of poison in a cup of water pollutes the whole cup. Please don't get me wrong, I'm not trying to bash people or religion. Satan is the one who is deceiving many people into praying to anyone and anything but God. Some religions teach praying to other people about 80 percent of the time, while giving God about 20 percent. This is me, and showing mercy confusion from the enemy.

I'm telling you this because I want to share with you what I read in the Bible.

The first commandment says, "I am the Lord thy God; Thou shalt have no other gods before Me."

The second commandment says, "Thou shalt not make unto thee any graven image or any likeness of anything that is in Heaven above, or that is in the earth beneath, or that is in the water under the earth. Thou shalt not bow down thyself to them: For I the Lord thy God am a jealous God, visiting the iniquity of the fathers upon the children unto the third and fourth generation of them that hate unto thousands of them that love Me, and keep My Commandments."

The Catholic church eliminated this second commandment and took the last Commandment and split it in half, making it still ten commandments. Remember what I said about Satan: he is the author of confusion and lies. He deceived people into taking away the second commandment. How many people would pray to all these false gods, people, saints, images, and so on if they knew the second commandment was ripped out? Anything to keep you from the Truth. By doing this, it opened the door for thousands of false religions. Anything to sway you from having a personal relationship with our Lord Jesus Christ, God, and the Holy Spirit of God. Remember, Jesus said "I am the way, the truth, and the life, No man comes to the Father but through Me" (John 14:6).

So, here it is: we we're taught to pray to all these saints. Paul, the Apostle had a lot to say about saints, and if you read the Epistles, you will learn a lot about saints, who are both here and in Heaven. If you are a Christian, you are a saint in God's eyes. God sees you as cleansed, washed, redeemed, sanctified, made holy, and a child of God. That's what saint means. Remember, we are not holy saints by our own works. We are our own works. We are holy and saints by what Jesus did for us to obtain salvation through Christ. "For by Grace are you saved through faith; and that not of yourselves: It is the gift of God. Not of works, lest any man should boast" (Ephesians 2:8-9).

Now you have a good understanding of saints, which is so much different than what some churches teach. If we believe the way these churches teach, then becoming a saint is all work related and that person gets all the glory. When we believe what the Bible really says about saints, then God gets all the glory, because salvation and Christianity is a free gift, given to us, so we give God all the glory.

CHAPTER 22
IS HEAVEN AND HELL REAL?

Jesus spoke more about Heaven and Hell more than anything else. If we're going to believe Jesus came on this earth, fulfilled all the prophecies, and came to set us free from Satan's power when we were gone astray, take our place and die on the cross in place of us for the forgiveness of our sins, then we must believe Him when He talked about Heaven and Hell. Here are some quotes Jesus said:

- "In my Father's house are many mansions: If it were not so, I would have told you so. I go to prepare a place for you; and if I go and prepare a place for you, I will come again, and receive you unto myself; that where I am, there ye may be also" (John 14:2-3).
- "And fear not them which kill the body, but are not able to kill the soul: but rather fear him which is able to destroy both soul and body in hell" (Matthew 10:28).
- "Men and brethren, let me freely speak unto you of the patriarch David, that he is both dead and buried, and his sepulcher is with us unto this day. Therefore, being a prophet, and knowing that God had sworn with an oath to

him, that of the fruit of his loins, according to the flesh, he would raise up Christ to sit on his throne. He seeing this before, spoke of the resurrection of Christ, that his soul was not left in hell, neither his flesh did see corruption. This Jesus hath God raised up, whereof we all are witnesses" (Acts 2:29-32).

I wanted to write these four scriptures to also show you that Jesus conquered death, Hell, and the grave for all those who come to Him and receive His free gift of salvation. The Bible says, "Call upon the Lord and thou shalt be Saved, and thy house." We were heading for eternal separation from God before we came to Jesus and asked Him into our heart and became followers of our Lord Jesus Christ. The gift of God is eternal life through Jesus Christ our Lord.

- "I am he that lives, and was dead; and behold, I am alive for evermore, and have the keys of hell and death" (Revelation 1:18).
- "Then said Jesus unto them, Verily, verily, I say unto you, I am the door of the sheep. All that ever came before me are thieves and robbers; but the sheep did not hear them. I am the door, by me, if any man enters in, he shall be saved, and shall go in and out and find pasture. The thief comes not, but for to steal, and kill, and to destroy: I am come that they might have life, and that they might have it more abundantly" (John 10:7-10).

Here, we just read that Jesus is the only way to Heaven. You can't get there any other way. When you go into a room, you open the door, and go through the doorway. Jesus just told us that He is the door to Heaven. Man will complicate things, but Jesus made it plain and simple. There are many scriptures that are mentioned in the Bible that talks about Heaven and Hell.

CHAPTER 23
IS LIMBO REAL? IF NOT, WHY DO SOME RELIGIONS TEACH THIS?

The Vatican abolished Limbo in 2007 at a time when abortions were being performed all over the world, and many people started asking questions, "Will the baby spend eternity away from God?" The doctrine of Limbo was taught for many centuries, but it was abolished in 2007. It was taught that you had to hurry up and have your baby baptized into the church to escape Limbo. If the baby died before the baptism, then the baby would never get to see God or the parents. Limbo was said to be a place between Heaven and Hell. I believe this was put in their teachings to force parents to make the child a member of the Church. When abortion came into being so popular, women were getting extremely depressed, thinking the child would never be in Heaven with God. That's when in 2007 the Pope abolished the teaching of Limbo. Limbo was taught in their catechism for centuries.

CHAPTER 24

IS PURGATORY REAL? IF NOT, WHY DO SOME RELIGIONS TEACH ON THIS?

Purgatory was invented in the early eleventh century as a means for the church to control the new sources of income. Catholics were taught that you bought indulgences to shorten the time for your relative or friend suffering in Purgatory as you get cleansed of any sin, so that you will be pure as you enter Heaven. You would either buy a mass card or light a candle, and, the more you did this, the quicker that soul you are praying for got out and got to go to Heaven sooner.

Although the sale of indulgences was abolished in 1567, the church still accepted money as an offering instead of a sale. Jesus shed his blood for the forgiveness of your sins. All the money in the world cannot buy forgiveness and help us get to Heaven. Only the blood atonement of our Lord Jesus Christ has the power to take away sin. The Bible says in Hebrews 9:22, "And almost, all things are by the law purged with blood, and without shedding of blood is no remission." In the Old Testament, the blood of animals was sacrificed, and sin was only covered. In the New Testament, Jesus' blood totally takes away sin. Jesus was predicted hundreds of times in the old testament about the Savior who was to come and save us from our sins and deliver us from Satan's power when we were gone astray. John the Baptist announced Jesus when he said, "Behold the Lamb of God which is come to take away the sins of the world." I mentioned this because I want you to understand that all the money in the world, and purgatory can never cleanse you of sin. Only Jesus can forgive and save you, make you clean and bring you to Heaven.

In 2017, Pope Francis abolished the places where souls were supposed to go after death. This came when abortion was running rampant and mothers were going to confession extremely depressed over the baby, wondering where the baby's soul went.

Jesus said that the little children go to Heaven if they die, and never said anything about Limbo or Purgatory. Jesus was dedicated in the temple as a child. Baptism comes when you are old enough to make that decision to follow Christ on your own. Being baptized into a church isn't the way to Salvation.

Salvation comes when we believe on the Lord Jesus Christ and turn to Him. Jesus said in the Gospels little children go to Heaven when they die. Religions have a way of making up laws, rules, and regulations to suit their own profits. There's a big difference between religion and salvation. The building isn't the church. The people are the church. The building is a place where the church gathers together to Praise and worship God and learn His Holy Word, the Bible. The book of Psalms is a great book to read and learn how the people of God prayed and sang unto the Lord throughout the ages. I think Psalms is a great book to read when you feel down.

CHAPTER 25

SHOULD WE PRAY FOR PEOPLE WHO HAVE ALREADY PASSED ON? IF NOT, WHY DO RELIGIONS TEACH US THAT WE SHOULD?

I can't stress it enough. I know I've said it many times in my books that it all boils down to one thing. Satan is out to trick people into praying to anyone, as long as it's not praying to God the Father, Jesus, or the Holy Spirit. Jesus said that when He goes away, He will send the Comforter, the Holy Spirit; and He will guide you into all Truth (John 16:7). Jesus also said ask the Father in my name.

"I am the way, the truth, and the life, No man comes unto the Father but by me." In other words, no other way but through Jesus.

Okay, let's get to the question. Should we pray for dead people? The Bible doesn't say we go into a temporary place. Wherever we go, it will be eternal; so, praying for someone after they die isn't scriptural. We can and should pray for our loved ones before they meet God.

- "It is appointed unto man once to die, then after this, the judgment" (Hebrews 9:27).
- Luke 16:26 says, "Besides all this, between us and you, there is a great gulf fixed: so that they which

would pass from here to you cannot; neither can they pass to us, that would come from there."

These are the words of Christ letting us know that we can't hear them, and they can't hear us. We can't bail people out once they are there. It's one place or the other forever. This is why I stress praying for your loved ones *before* they die.

I can recall many times when I either lost something or forgot something, I asked the Holy Spirit to find or remember something and thanked God for showing me. I remember as a child in confirmation class, the teacher telling me to ask Saint Anthony for help whenever you lose something. This is not in the Bible and is unscriptural. No person that has passed on hears or answers our prayers. This is a trick of Satan to divert you from praying to God. This is why I want I want you to know how important it is to pray for your loved ones now! Not after they die when it's too late. We go to one place or the other, and there's no in between.

Religions can be so confusing sometimes. Why not pray for someone before they die? I know I'm repeating myself, but I just want to stress how important this subject is. Give your love now while he or she is still here. Send cards, give flowers, compliment them, help them, and just being there means a lot. Show your love now. Pray for them and show them the Jesus you know. Don't wait until their gone. Do these things now! You will be a great help to that person, and you will not have any regrets when they are gone. In Heaven, they will thank you for your love and dedication to Christ's teachings. I don't tell you all these things to down anyone. I tell you this because God loves you, and so do I.

CHAPTER 26
WHY SHOULD WE LOVE AND PRAY FOR OUR ENEMIES? WHAT GOOD WILL THAT DO FOR ME?

Let me start out with this question to you!

Can you count the number of times you asked God to forgive you? What were you like before you became a Christian?

When we love and pray for our enemies, we are showing love to that person and not to the problem. Look at it this way: we are being controlled by good or evil. When Jesus was here on this earth 2000 years ago, He understood them better than they understood themselves. He delivered people from bondage. Jesus prayed to the Father for His enemies and prayed, "Forgive them Father, for they know not what they do" (Luke 23:34). Jesus understood that these people were under the control of Satan and didn't even know it. We should look at people like Jesus did, and try to reach out like He did.

Like I said in another chapter, it's actually doing us good, too. Because by doing this, it shows that we are not holding any unforgiveness toward that person we choose to love and pray for. Choose to love because hate and unforgiveness destroys. That's why Jesus said, love your enemies; because if you hate your enemies, you have no way to redeem them and see your enemies transformed. If you love your enemies, you will discover that at the very root of love is the power of redemption.

Jesus said

> You have heard that it has been said, thou shalt love thy neighbor and hate your enemies; But I say unto you, love your enemies, bless them that curse you, do good to them that hate you, and pray for them which despitefully use you and persecute you. That you may be the children of your Father which is in heaven: for he makes his sun to rise on the evil and the good, and sends rain on the just and the unjust. For if you love them which love you, what reward have you? Do not the publicans the same?
>
> (Matthew 5:43-46)

I thank God that, before I was a Christian, the sun still shined on me every day as Jesus said, "He makes the sun to rise on the evil and the good and sends rain on the just and unjust."

- "Be ye therefore merciful as your Father also is merciful" (Luke 6:36).
- "Beloved, let us love one another; for love is of God, and every one that loves is born of God and knows God. He that loves not knows not God, for God is Love" (1 John 4:7).
- "A new Commandment I give unto you, that you love one another, as I have loved you, that you also love one another. By this all men know that you are my disciples, if you have love one for another" (John 13:34-35).
- "Bless them which persecute you: Bless and curse not. Rejoice with them that do rejoice, and weep with them that weep. Be of the same mind one

toward another. Mind not high things, but condescend to men of low estate. Be not wise in your own conceits. Recompense to no man evil for evil. Provide things honest in the sight of all men. If it be possible, as much as lies in you, live peaceably with all men. Dearly beloved, avenge not yourselves, but rather give place unto wrath: for it is written, vengeance is mine, I will repay says the Lord. Therefore if thine enemy hunger, feed him. If he is thirsty, give him drink: for in so doing, thou shalt heap coals of fire on his head. Be not overcome of evil but overcome evil with good" (Romans 12:14-21).

- "Let all things be done with Charity (Love)" (1 Corinthians 16:14).

- "Rejoice not when your enemy falls, and let not your heart be glad when he stumbles: Lest the Lord see it, and it displease him, and he turn away his wrath from him" (Proverbs 14:17-18).

- "He that is slow to wrath is of great understanding: but he that is hasty of spirit exalts folly" (Proverbs 14:29).

- "If thine enemy be hungry, give him bread to eat; and if he be thirsty, give him water to drink. For thou shalt heap coals of fire on his head and the Lord shall reward you" (Proverbs 25:21-22).

CHAPTER 27
I HEAR THAT THERE ARE DIFFERENT TYPES OF LOVE. WHAT ARE THEY?

There are three types of Love we see in the Bible.

1. *Eros* love - The type of love that resembles romantic love.
2. *Philia* love - Brotherly love, family showing loyalty, showing appreciation, high moral principles toward each other.
3. *Agape* love - A love we have for everyone; willingness to help without a reward and doing good deeds for people. Showing God's love. A love inside us we give freely to others regardless of our relationship to them. The whole idea of *Agape* love is that we don't need to have met them before we still want to help them.

Eros love should never come before *Philia* and *Agape* love.

Love is a verb: an action word. Looking at someone and deciding that you want to love them, even when they mess up, even when they fall down, even when they're not the same person, even when they fight with you or make you cry. Love is making a choice every day to love someone. There is a difference between feeling love for someone, such as caring about a person, and loving someone—*choosing* to love that person. Love is an action word.

If you marry someone only because they are beautiful, you are in for a rude awakening, because nobody is perfect. We all have flaws. Balance is a great attribute to have when you are seeking a wife or husband. Beauty is nice, but you must look at who the person is also.

- "Favor is deceitful and beauty is vain, but a woman that fears the Lord, she shall be praised" (Proverbs 31:30).
- "Who can find a virtuous woman? For her price is above rubies" (Proverbs 31:10).

The same can go for the man. A godly man is worth more than rubies to the woman seeking a godly husband.

There is no better place to find all the types of love than in The Bible. The more you learn about God, the more you learn about Love.

CHAPTER 28
ARE THERE ANGELS HERE ON EARTH?

There are many great stories written all throughout the Bible that mentions Angels here on earth.

- "Then the devil left Jesus, and behold, Angels came and ministered unto Him" (Matthew 4:11).

- "And without controversy, great is the mystery of godliness: God was manifest in the flesh, justified in the Spirit, seen of Angels, preached unto the Gentiles, believed on in the world, received up into Glory" (1 Timothy 3:16).

- "And the Angels of the Lord said unto Elijah, go down with him; Be not afraid of him. And he arose and went down with him unto the King" (2 Kings 1:15).

- "Then said I, O my Lord, what are these? And the Angel that talked with me said unto me, I will show you what these are" (Zechariah 1:9)

- "And the Angel answering said unto him, I am Gabriel, that stand in the presence of God; and am sent to speak unto you; and to show you these glad tidings" (Luke 1:19).

- "And the Angel of the Lord spoke unto Philip saying arise, and go toward the south unto the way that goes down from Jerusalem unto Gaza which is desert" (Acts 8:26)

- "For He shall give his Angels charge over thee to keep thee in all thy way. They shall bear thee up in their hands lest thou dash thy foot against a stone" (Psalms 91:11-12).
- "My God has sent his Angel, and has shut the lion's mouths that they have not hurt me: forasmuch as before him innocence was found in me; and also before you O King, have I done no hurt" (Daniel 6:22).
- "But the Angel of the Lord opened the prison doors, and brought them forth, and said; Go, stand and speak in the Temple to the people all the words of this life" (Acts 5:19-20).
- "Are they not all ministering spirits sent forth to minister for them who shall be heirs of Salvation?" (Hebrews 1:14).
- "And immediately the Angel of the Lord smote him because he gave not God the glory" (Acts 12:23).

So here we have it. Angels are here on earth. One thing I want to mention here though, is that angels are not supposed to be worshiped or prayed to. Nobody is to be worshipped except God. God loves you. Let me put it this way: you have children, and most of the time whenever your children want to ask you something, they go over to the next door neighbor and ask them to ask you a question; or your children call their uncle on the phone right in front of you and ask him to ask you a question or request. They speak to you once in a while, but mostly through someone else. How would that make you feel? You see, God is your Father, and you are His child if you accepted the Lord Jesus Christ into your heart. When I say heart, I mean life. So, this is why I really wanted to teach you on this matter concerning angels and saints. I will end it with these scriptures.

- "And I fell at his feet to worship him. And he said unto me, see thou do it not: I am thy fellow servant and of thy brethren that have the testimony of God" (Revelations 19:10).
- "And I John saw these things, and heard them. And when I had heard and seen, I fell down to worship before the feet of the Angel which showed me these things. Then he said unto me; See thou do it not. There are many examples of Angels on assignments from God, not only in the Bible but also people throughout history witnessed encounters with Angels" (Revelations 22:8-9).

It's very important to know the Word of God; the Bible; because Satan can appear as an angel of light and deceive you into praying to anyone but God.

CHAPTER 29
WHAT IS THE MEANING OF CHURCH TO YOU? IS IT THE BUILDING YOU GO TO? OR IS IT THE PEOPLE?

"And if he shall neglect to hear them, tell it unto the church: But if he refuses to hear the church, let him be unto thee as a heathen man and a publican" (Matthew 18:17).

So here we have Jesus saying go to the church. When He said go to the church, He wasn't saying talk to the building. He was saying talk to the people which is the church. So now we see that the Christians are the church.

"Take heed therefore unto yourselves, and to all the flock, over the which the Holy Spirit has made you overseers, to feed the church of God, which he has purchased with his own blood" (Acts 20:28). Here, it is not saying feed the building. It is saying feed the church. The building is simply a building where the church can gather together in prayer, teaching, ministry, and fellowship.

- "Likewise greet the church which is in their house" (Romans 16:5).
- "Husbands, love your wives, even as Christ also loved the church, and gave himself for it" (Ephesians 5:25).

- "And he is the head of the body, the church: who is the beginning, the firstborn from the dead, that in all things he might have the preeminence" (Colossians 1:8).

These are just a few scriptures that help you to understand that the church is the people; and the people are the church.

CHAPTER 30
WHY ARE THERE PEOPLE WHO SAY THEY ARE BORN AGAIN? WHAT DOES BORN AGAIN MEAN?

I've visited many denominations since becoming a Christian over fifty years ago. There are some people who call themselves Christians, but don't use the term saved or born again; however, Jesus used these terms many times in the Gospels. Some denominations will frown on the phrases, born again or saved, and instead use the terms such as a life changing experience, or made a decision to follow Christ, or just say they are Christian. Jesus gave us these names born again, saved, and Christ follower. The Apostles Paul and Peter quoted some scriptures also to help us understand these names.

- "Jesus answered and said unto him; Verily, Verily, I say unto you, except a man be Born Again, He cannot see the Kingdom of God. Nicodemus said unto Jesus, how can a man be born again when he is old? Can he enter the second time into his mother's womb, and be born?" Jesus answered, Verily, Verily I say unto thee, except a man be born of the water and of the Spirit, he cannot enter into the Kingdom of God. That which is born of the flesh is flesh, and that which is born of the Spirit is spirit. Marvel not that I said unto thee; You must be Born Again. The wind blows where it wishes and you hear the sound thereof, but cannot tell when it comes and where it goes; so is every one that is born of the Spirit" (John 3:3-8).

- "Blessed be the God and Father of our Lord Jesus Christ which according to His abundant mercy, has begotten us (again) unto a lively hope by the resurrection of Jesus Christ from the dead" (1 Peter 1:3).

- "Being Born Again, not of corruptible seed, but of incorruptible, by the Word of God which lives and abides forever" (1 Peter 1:23)

- "Therefore, if any man be in Christ, he is a new creature: Old things are passed away and behold, all things are become new" (2 Corinthians 5:17).

- "And you hath he quickened, who were dead in trespasses and sins" (Ephesians 2:1).

Quickened means to make alive; to verify, to revive or resuscitate, as from death or an inanimate state; so, quickening denotes giving life or energy to something or someone. When someone says they are born again, that's what they mean. "[Getting Baptized] Buried with Him (Jesus) in baptism, wherein also you are risen with Him through the faith of the operation of God, who has raised Jesus from the dead" (Colossians 2:21).

Baptism in water is a public profession of your faith in Christ and going into the water, laying down your old life and coming up out of the water as a new person in Christ. So, there you have it. Being born again means you have a whole new life, once you come to Jesus and receive Him as your Lord and Savior. Jesus paid the penalty for our sins and when we ask Jesus to forgive us and come and live in us, He will, and gives us a whole new life.

I hope this helped you to understand what born again means.

CHAPTER 31
PEOPLE TELL ME THEY ARE SAVED. WHAT DOES SAVED MEAN?

To me, saved means Jesus Christ has rescued me from the judgment and wrath of God when I called upon the Lord and received Jesus as my Lord and Savior. Romans 6:23 says, "For the wages of sin is death, but the gift of God is Eternal Life through Jesus Christ our Lord."

So, what does saved mean? It means saved from eternal separation from God, and death eternal in Hell, but the gift of God is eternal life through Jesus Christ our Lord.

Here are some scriptures to help you get a good understanding of what saved is:

- "And she shall bring forth a son, and thou shalt call his name Jesus, for he shall save his people from their sins" (Matthew 1:21).
- "When his disciples heard of it, they were exceedingly angered, saying, who then can be saved?" (Matthew 19:25).
- "He saved others; himself he cannot save. If he be the King of Israel, let him now come down from the cross, and we will believe him" (Matthew 27:42).

I believe the people that were saying that were being led of Satan, because Satan and these people knew the scriptures. They knew the Savior of the world was here according to the scriptures, and Jesus knew that this was needed to be done to save us from sin and damnation as John the Baptist proclaimed: "Behold, the Lamb of God which takes away the sins of the world" (John 1:29).

The devil knew this and used these people to try and get Jesus to come down off the cross. Just before Jesus died on that cross, He cried, "It is finished" (John 19:30).

"And they that passed by railed on him, wagging their heads, saying, Ah, thou that destroys the temple, and will build it in three days, Save thyself, and come down from the cross. Likewise also the chief priests mocking said among themselves with the scribes, He saved others, himself he cannot save" (Mark 15:29-31).

The devil tried but failed.

- "And they that heard it said, who then can be saved? And he said, the things which are impossible with man are possible with God" (Luke 18:26-27).

- "But I (Jesus) receive not testimony from man: but these things I say, that you might be Saved" (John 5:34).

- "Jesus said- For God sent not his Son into the world to condemn the world, but that the world through him might be Saved" (John 3:17).

- "And they continuing daily with one accord in the temple, and breaking bread from house to house, did eat their meat with gladness of heart. Praising God, and having favor with the people, and the Lord added to the church daily such as should be Saved" (Acts 2:46-47).

- "And brought them out and said, what must I do to be Saved. And they said, believe on the Lord Jesus Christ and thou shalt be Saved, and thy house. That's a wonderful promise (and thy house)" (Acts 16:30-31)

Paul said in Romans, "For I speak to you Gentiles Inasmuch as I am the Apostle of the Gentiles, I magnify mine office. If by any means I may provoke to emulation them which are my flesh (Jewish,) and might Save some of them" (Romans 11:13-14).

- "If you confess with your mouth the Lord Jesus and shall believe in your heart that God raised him (Jesus) from the dead, thou shalt be Saved. For with the heart man believes unto righteousness, and with the mouth confession is made unto Salvation" (Romans 10:9-10).
- "For whosoever shall call upon the name of the Lord shall be Saved" (Romans 10:13).
- "For the preaching of the cross is to them that perish foolishness; but unto us which are Saved, it is the power of God" (1 Corinthians 1:18).
- "But after the kindness and love of God our Savior toward man appeared, Not by works of righteousness which we have done, but according to his mercy, he Saved us by the washing of regeneration and renewing of the Holy Spirit. Which he shed on us abundantly through Jesus Christ our Savior" (Titus 3:4-6).

- "Let him know that he which converts the sinner from the error of his way shall Save a soul from death and shall hide a multitude of sins" (James 5:20).
- Again, Romans 10:13 says, "For whosoever shall call upon the name of the Lord (shall be saved)."

I hope these scriptures gave you a better understanding of being saved.

CHAPTER 32

IS IT OK FOR CHRISTIANS TO HAVE A CARREER IN POLITICS? IS VOTING CONSIDERED TOO WORLDLY FOR CHRISTIANS?

I met many Christians throughout my fifty years of teaching the Bible that don't vote because they think that getting involved in politics would be too worldly. This is very sad. All I can say about this is that, if every Christian thought that way, our government would be a communist socialist ungodly government. Christians would be persecuted just like in other socialist countries. Our churches would be turned into government warehouses or torn down. Christians in other countries are thrown into prison for their Faith. Our Bibles would be taken away from us, and anything Christian hanging on our walls would be taken from us. Christian schools would be closed, and this is just a little of what would happen to us here in our country if we don't have good decent Christians working in our government.

Voting is so important if you want to be free to practice your Christian faith. There are way too many Christians that don't vote, and if they did, America wouldn't have these problems we see today. Don't let the devil sway you from voting. As I mention in my other book, *The Recurring Dream*: There are two paths. Which one are you on? One leads to life and peace, and the other leads to bondage and ungodliness. If we end up having a socialist government, all our freedoms will be taken away from us as I just mentioned. Sometimes we need to read something more than once to get us to think. I can't stress it enough how important and right it is to vote. If you don't vote and enjoy living a Christian life, you have that privilege because another Christian is voting for values.

Here are some scriptures to help you have a better understanding of the importance of Christians working in Government and Christians voting: "When the righteous are in authority, the people rejoice: but when the wicked bears rule the people mourn" (Proverbs 29:2).

Candidates or proposals that violate the Bible's commands for life, family, or faith should never be supported. We all know there are two parties: Democratic or Republican, and it doesn't take a rocket scientist to see what each party stands for. One party is taking God out of our lives in every way possible from child to adult. The other party is trying hard to restore what the enemy has stolen from us. In my opinion, every Christian that doesn't vote is giving the enemy one more vote.

Here are some more scriptures on Christians voting.

- "Blessed is the nation whose God is the Lord; the people whom he hath chosen for his inheritance" (Psalms 33:12)
- "The wicked shall be turned into hell, and all the nations that forget God" (Psalm 9:17).

So: What does this scripture have to do with voting? I'm glad you asked.

I would say a lot. You may have two people running for something in government. One may have no regard for Christianity, and the other may be a Christian and has a love for God. Some may think you can't mix religion and politics but remember the two scriptures I just wrote. If you want to refresh your thoughts on this, read them again.

I hope this helped you have a better understanding of why Christians must vote if they want to be able to live a Christian life and have the freedom to be who they want to be and do what they want to do. If we don't vote, then we can't complain if we lose our freedom through liberalism and communism.

CHAPTER 33
IS IT NECESSARY TO GO TO CHURCH ON A REGULAR BASIS?

The Apostle Paul taught in one of his messages to the church of the Thessalonians on this subject in the book of Hebrews.

- "Let us hold fast to the profession of our Faith without wavering; for he is faithful that promised. And let us consider one another to provoke unto Love and to good works; Not forsaking the assembling of ourselves together, as the manner of some is, but exhorting one another, and so much the more, as you see the day approaching" (Hebrews 19:23-25).

- "Jesus said, Go ye therefore and teach all nations, baptizing them in the name of the Father, and of the Son, and of the Holy Spirit. Teaching them to observe all things whatsoever I have commanded you: and Lo, I am with you always, even unto the end of the world. Amen" (Matthew 28:18-20).

- "Then they that gladly received his word were baptized: and the same day there were added unto them about three thousand souls. And they continued steadfastly in the Apostles doctrine and fellowship, and in breaking of bread and in prayers" (Acts 2:41).

We get great teachings at church services. We grow in our Faith at church services.

Gathering together to be with other believers is a time of celebration. We celebrate our Christianity in praise and thanksgiving to God for what our Lord Jesus Christ has done for us. We also gather together to learn the Word of God, the Bible. The church building is also like a spiritual hospital where we can be prayed for, encouraged, built up in the faith, a place where we can get good guidance in so many areas of our life; where we can hear the Word of God that will free us of so many things the enemy brings on people such as brokenness, loneliness, sin, guilt, heartbreak, anxiety, hurt, unforgiveness, depression, etc. Going to a good Bible-believing, Bible-teaching, Christ-centered church will encourage you in your walk with the Lord. A Christ-centered church will help you grow in the faith. God ordains people to be pastors and teachers for His church.

Remember! A building is a building where the Church gathers together in fellowship, teaching, learning, praise, and worship, healing, and prayer, and salvation.

CHAPTER 34
IS IT NECESSARY TO READ THE BIBLE AND PRAY?

Is it necessary for us to eat food and drink water? Of course! If we eat a good healthy diet every day, live in a clean environment, then we have a great chance of our body being good and healthy. If we only eat one meal a day and very little water, eventually our body will deteriorate and die. It's the same way with our soul. We must feed our soul with the Word of God. Jesus said, "(It is written) Man shall not live by bread alone, but by every word that proceeds out of the mouth of God" (Matthew 4:4).

This shows us that it is very important that we read the Bible every day. The Bible is the living Word of God. If you haven't been reading or don't know where to start, I would say read the four Gospels to start. Even if it's just one chapter. After time, you will develop a hunger to read more each day. The Gospel of John is a great place to start. I've heard people say, as they began to read that the words just popped out, and they could feel the Spirit and love of God embracing them in His love. Now concerning prayer: is it necessary to pray? Let me ask you, is it necessary to talk to your husband or your wife? What kind of relationship would you have if you thought, *Oh, I talked a few days ago. I don't need to talk to you for a while.* How would your relationship be? God calls us His children and the Bride of Christ.

101

Husbands, love your wives even as Christ loved the church and gave himself for it. That he might sanctify it and cleanse it with the washing of the water by the Word that he might present it to himself as a glorious church, not having spot or wrinkle, or any such thing; but that it should be holy and without blemish. so ought men to love their wives as their own bodies. He that loves his wife loves himself. For no man ever yet hated his own flesh; but nourishes and cherishes it, even as the Lord the Church. For we are members of his flesh and of his bones. For this cause shall a man leave his father and mother, and shall be joined unto his wife, and they two shall be one flesh. This is a great mystery: but I speak concerning Christ and the Church.

Ephesians 5:25-32

So here we have it. Paul the Apostle is saying the Church is the Bride of Christ. Jesus loves you, and He wants to hear from you. The best way to hear from Him is through His Word.

- "Let us be glad and rejoice and give honor to Him: for the marriage of the Lamb is come, and his wife hath made herself ready. And to her was granted that she should be arrayed in fine linen, clean and white, for the fine linen is the righteousness of saints. And he said unto me, Write, Blessed, are they which are called unto the marriage supper of the Lamb, and he said unto me These are the true sayings of God" (Revelation 19:7-9).

Getting back to the question: is it necessary to pray? Yes! It's very important. If you feel as though you don't know how to pray, or just don't know what to pray, The book of Psalms is a great book on prayers. God called The Psalmist David a man after His own heart. David had faults and was not considered some big holy priest. As a matter of fact, he started out as a sheepherder, which was considered a job of low esteem in those days, but God raised him up to be a king. Although David got into sin, which caused him to make some very bad choices in his life. He called out to God in his troubles and developed a great relationship with God in his repentance and confessions to God. As you read his 150 Psalms, you will be able to relate them with your own life as you talk with your Heavenly Father. The Psalms will help you in all these situations. I hope this helped you to understand the importance of Prayer and reading the The Psalmist David said, "Thy Word is a lamp unto my feet, and a light unto my path" (Psalm 119:105).

CHAPTER 35
HOW DO I HEAR FROM GOD?

There are many ways we hear from God. I would say the surest way to hear from God, would be through the reading of God's Word, the Bible. We can also hear from God through people who are mature in the Lord, such as a pastor, a Bible teacher, a friend, someone preaching. Also, the words to Christian music on TV, radio, or internet, or by reading a devotional may be exactly what you needed to hear. God can speak His Love and Peace through the beauty of nature.

- "The Heavens declare the Glory of God, and the firmament shows His handywork. Day unto day utters speech, and night unto night shows knowledge" (Psalms 19:1-2).
- Psalms 119:105 is worth mentioning again, which says, "Thy Word is a lamp unto my feet, and a light unto my path."
- "But he answered and said, It is written, Man shall not live by bread alone, but by every word that proceeds out of the mouth of God" (Matthew 4:4).
- "Let the Word of Christ dwell in you richly in all wisdom; teaching and admonishing one another in Psalms and Hymns, and Spiritual Songs,

singing with Grace in your hearts to the Lord"
(Colossians 3:16).

I heard from God many times through all the ways I mentioned here. The Holy Spirit is our Counselor and Guide, our Comforter. Many times' it is that still small voice that knocks on the door of our heart.

Jesus said,

- I will pray the Father, and he shall give you another comforter that he may dwell with you forever. Even the Spirit of Truth; whom the world cannot receive, because it sees him not; but you know him, for he dwells in you, and shall be in you. I will not leave you comfortless; I will come to you. But the Comforter which is the Holy Spirit, whom the Father will send in my name, he shall teach you all things, and bring to remembrance, whatsoever I have said unto you" (John 14:16-19).

- "Nevertheless I am continually with you: You have holden me by my right hand. You will guide me with thy counsel, and afterward receive me to glory" (Psalms 73:23-24).

- "And the Lord shall guide thee continually, and satisfy thy soul in drought, and make fat thy bones, and thou shalt be like a watered garden, and like a spring of water, whose waters fail not" (Isaiah 58:11).

- "Howbeit, when he, the Spirit of truth is come, he will guide you into all truth; for he shall not speak of himself; but whatsoever he shall hear, that shall he speak: and he will show you things to come" (John 16:13).

These are just a few scriptures from the Bible. There are a lot more, and as you read God's Word, you will find more and more treasures.

CHAPTER 36
WHAT IS A BABY CHRISTIAN?

None of us are born Christian. There comes a time when we make a decision to be a Christian on our own, a Christ follower. That could be any age from age of accountability to the last minutes of our old age. In other words, if someone is ninety years old and just decided to call upon the Lord and ask Jesus into his or her heart, then they are a Christian just starting out on their journey as a Baby Christian. If someone is twenty years old and has been a Christian for ten years living for the Lord, then that person is actually older in the Lord than the person who is ninety years old who just became a Christian a few months ago. Here are some scriptures to help you understand what I just wrote.

1 Corinthians 3:1-3 is one example. Here is the Apostle Paul is teaching the church of the Corinthians, and he is saying that he can't get too deep on his messages because the church was just starting. The people were new converts. Paul knew that you don't give steak to a newborn baby. Instead, you feed the baby milk (the milk of the Word):

> "And I brethren could not speak unto you as unto spiritual, but as unto carnal, even as unto babes in Christ. I have fed you with milk, and not with meat; for hitherto ye were not able to bear it; neither yet now are ye able. Foe ye are yet carnal; for whereas there is

among you envying and strife, and divisions, are ye not carnal, and walk as men?'"

Here are some more scriptures:

- "For when for the time you should to be teachers, ye have need that someone teach you again which be the first principles of the oracles of God; and are become such as have need of milk and not of strong meat. For everyone that uses milk is unskillful in the word of righteousness; for he is a babe. But strong meat belongs to them that are of full age, even those who by reason of use have their senses exercised to decern both good and evil" (Hebrews 5:12-14).

- "Wherefore laying aside all malice, and all guile, and hypocrisies, and envies, and all evil speaking, As newborn babes, desire the sincere milk of the word that ye may grow thereby: If so be ye have tasted that the Lord is gracious" (1 Peter 2:1-3).

Here in this next verse Jesus is praying and giving thanks to God the Father for revealing the Word of God to babes in Christ in front of these Priests that spent their whole life as a Priest but refused to know the Truth concerning Jesus; being the Savior of the world, and revealed this to babes in Christ. "In that Jesus rejoiced in Spirit and said, I thank thee O Father, Lord of heaven and earth, that you have hid these things from the wise and prudent, and has revealed them unto babes, even so Father; for so it seemed good in thy sight" (Luke 10:21).

There are more scriptures on this, and you will find them as you read more and learn more of God's Word.

Let me add one more thing to this question. There are priests and pastors who have the title of priest or pastor but graduated from a seminary or college that teaches so many things that are unscriptural and come out knowing less than when they first started. Not all Christian colleges and seminaries teach sound doctrine. Do a serious research before entering any Bible School.

CHAPTER 37
WHY DO SOME PEOPLE THINK IT IS FOOLISH TO BE A CHRISTIAN, OR THINK CHRISTIANS ARE TOO BORING?

Some people think being a Christian will be too boring because they don't give God a chance. Jesus promises a life so much more fulfilling than what people had before being a Christian. Satan is out to kill, steal, and destroy. He will tell you anything to keep you from living the life Jesus wants you to have. Satan will put thoughts in your head and try to make you think living a Christ filled life is foolish. He will try and get you to believe that you will lose what you have. Jesus doesn't take anything from us. As we grow in our faith, we may let go of things that are not good, but Jesus blesses us beyond what we think is good when we live for Him. He knows us better than we know ourselves. Jesus has a much better life to offer than the world Satan has to offer. Everything Satan puts before you will bring death and destruction and steal what God has for you. Where does loneliness, sickness, poverty, death, destruction, confusion, fear, spiritual blindness, hate, envy, unforgiveness, immorality, fighting, etc. come from? It comes from Satan, the enemy of your soul.

Where does love, peace, joy, life, forgiveness, purity, calmness, charity, hope, vision, prosperity, talent, friendships, etc. come from? It all comes from God. God is love. Here are some scriptures to help you understand why some people will believe the lies of Satan that being a Christian is foolish.

Here the Apostle Paul is preaching to the Corinthian:

> For Christ sent me not to baptize, but to preach the gospel: not with wisdom of words, lest the cross of Christ should be made of none effect. For the preaching of the cross is to them that perish foolishness; but unto us which are saved, it is the power of God. For it is written, I will destroy the wisdom of the wise, and will bring to nothing the understanding of the prudent. Where is the wise? Where is the scribe? Where is the disputer of this world? Has not God made foolish the wisdom of this world? For after that in the wisdom of God the world by wisdom knew not God by the foolishness of preaching to save them that believe. For the Jews require a sign and the Greeks seek after wisdom. But we preach Christ crucified, unto the Jews a stumbling block, and unto the Greeks foolishness. But unto them which are called both Jews and Greeks, Christ the power of God and the wisdom of God.Because the foolishness of God is wiser than men; and the weakness of God is stronger than men. For you see your calling, brethren, how that not many wise men after the flesh, not many noble, are called.But God has chosen the foolish things of the world to confound the wise; and God has chosen the weak things of the world to confound the things which are mighty.
>
> 1 Corinthians 1:17-27

I'm happy I can say I am one of the foolish God uses to confound the wise of this world. The world may think the

Bible to be foolish or Christianity foolish, but it's just the opposite. It's very wise to be a believer in Christ. If you do decide to go to a Bible college, make sure you do some good research on their beliefs, because there are some good ones and there are some that teach things that are contrary to the teachings of Christ and the apostles. There are some good places, but you will have to do some good research if you are planning on going to a Christian college.

CHAPTER 38
HOW CAN I KNOW THAT GOD REALLY LOVES ME?

This may seem like a very simple question, but to many people it may not. Some may think that there is no God, or some may be deceived into believing in some false god. If you were to ask some people this question; they may not know. It could be no one ever told them. Many false religions are handed down from generation to generation. This is one reason why Jesus told his Apostles so many times to go and teach all nations.

- "Go and teach all nations baptizing them in the name of the Father, and of the Son, and of the Holy Spirit, teaching them to observe all things whatsoever I have commanded you; and Lo, I am with you always, even unto the end of the world, Amen" (Matthew 28:19-20).

- "And he (Jesus) said unto them; Go ye into all the world, and preach the Gospel to every creature "The Spirit of the Lord is upon me, because he has anointed me to preach the Gospel to the poor, He has sent me to heal the brokenhearted, to preach deliverance to the captives, and recovering of sight to the blind, to set at liberty them that are bruised" (Luke 4:18).

So, getting back to the question, how do I know if God really loves me? The answer is in the scriptures. God loves you, and when Jesus came over 2000 years ago, He showed his great love for us in laying down His life for each and every one of us. As John the Baptist proclaimed: "Behold the Lamb of God which takes away the sin of the world."

God created the heavens and the earth, and all that is within it before creating man. In other words, God had us in mind and created everything first so it would all be ready for us when we come into the world. God loves you more than you can ever imagine.

Here are some beautiful scriptures that show you how much God really does love you:

- "For God so loved the world, that he gave his only begotten Son, that whosoever believes in Him should not perish, but have everlasting life For God sent not his Son into the world to condemn the world, but that the world through Him might be saved" (John 3:16-17).
- "Neither is their Salvation in any other: for there is none other name given under heaven given among men, whereby we must be saved" (Acts 4:12).
- "For I am not ashamed of the Gospel of Christ; for it is the power of God unto Salvation to everyone that believes; to the Jew first and also to the Greek" (Romans 1:16).
- "Nay, in all these things we are more than conquerors through Him that loved us. For I am persuaded that neither death, nor life, nor angels, nor principalities, nor things to come Nor height,

nor depth, nor any other creature, shall be able to separate us from the love of God, which is in Christ Jesus our Lord" (Romans 8:37-39).

- "But God, who is rich in mercy, for his great love wherewith he loved us Even when we were dead in sins, has quickened us together with Christ, (By Grace are you saved)" (Ephesians 2:4-5).

What Paul is saying here is that salvation is a free gift given to you. All we have to do is receive it by faith. You can't save yourself. Only Christ can cleanse us and make us clean and holy in His eyes through what Jesus done on the cross taking our sin and nailing it to the cross.

These are just a few scriptures, showing us that God loves you and has great plans for you. There are so many great promises and blessings all throughout the Bible and you will discover them as you read God's Word.

Jesus tells you to go and tell others what God has done for you, and what God can do for all those who come to Jesus.

As I bring my book to a close, I would like to share some great scriptures on love.

- "Beloved, let us love one another; for love is of God; and every one that loves is born of God, and knows God. He that loves not knows not God; for God is love. In this was manifested the love of God toward us, because that God sent his only begotten Son into the world that we might live through Him. Herein is love, not that we loved God, but that he loved us, and sent his Son to be the propitiation for our sins. Beloved, if God so loved us, we ought to love one another" (1 John 4:7-11).

- "I am the door: by me if any man shall enter, he shall be saved, and shall go in and out and find pasture. The thief comes to kill, steal, and destroy; I am come that they might have life, and that they might have it more abundantly. I am the good shepherd; the good shepherd gives his life for the sheep" (John 10:9-11).

- "I am the resurrection and the life; he that believes in me, though he were dead, yet shall he live. And whosoever lives and believes in me shall never die; Do you believe this?" (John 11:25-26).

- "A new commandment I give unto you, that you love one another; as I have loved you that you also love one another. By this shall all men know that you are my disciples, if you have love one to another" (John 13:34-35).

- Let not your heart be troubled: You believe in God, believe also in me. In my Father's house are many mansions: If it were not so, I would have told you. I go and prepare a place for you. And if I go and prepare a place for you, I will come again and receive you unto myself, that where I am, there you may be also. And wherever I go you know, and the way you know. Thomas said unto him, Lord, we know not where you are going; and how can we know the way? Jesus said unto him, I am the Way, the Truth, and the Life: no man comes unto the Father, but through me. If you had known me, you should have known my Father also, and from henceforth (from this time on) you know him, and have seen him. Philip said unto him Lord, show us the Father, and it will satisfy us. Jesus said unto him: Have I been so long time with you, and yet you have not known me; Philip? He that has seen me has seen the Father; and how do you say then, show us the Father? You believe not that I am in the Father, and the Father in me? The words that I speak unto you I speak not of myself; but the Father that dwells in me, he does the works. Believe me, that I am in the Father, and the Father in me; or else believe me for the very works sake. Truly truly I say unto you, He that believes on me, the works that I do shall he do also; and greater works than these shall he do; because I go unto my Father. And whatsoever you shall ask in my name, that will I do, that the Father may be glorified in the Son. If you ask anything in my name, I will do it. If you love me, keep my Commandments. And I will pray the Father and he shall give you another Comforter, that he may abide with you forever. Even the Spirit of Truth, whom the world cannot receive, because it sees him not, neither knows him, but you know him; for he dwells in you, and shall be in you. I will not leave you comfortless; I will come to you. Yet a little while, and the world will see me no more; but you see me; because I live, you shall live also. At that day, you shall know that I am in the Father, and you in me, and I in you. He that has my Commandments, and keeps them, he it is that loves me; and he that loves me shall be loved of my Father, and I will love him, and will manifest myself to him. Judas said unto him (not Iscariot) Lord, how is it that you will manifest thyself unto us and not unto the world? Jesus answered and said unto him, if a man loves me, he will keep my words; and my Father will love him, and we will come unto him, and make our abode with him. He that loves me not, keeps not my sayings; and the word which you hear is not mine; but the Father's which sent me. These things have I spoken unto you, being yet present with you. But the comforter, which is the Holy Spirit, whom the Father will send in my name, He shall teach you all things, and bring all things to your remembrance, whatsoever I have said unto you. Peace I leave with you, My Peace I give unto you; not as the world gives, I give unto you; Let not your heart be troubled, neither let it be afraid. You have heard how I said unto you, I go away, and come again unto you, If you love me, you would rejoice, because I said, I go unto the Father, for my Father is greater than I. And now I have told you before it come to pass, that when it is come to pass, you might believe. Hereafter, I will not talk much with you; for the prince of this world comes, and has nothing in me. But that the world may know that I love the Father, and as the Father gave me Commandment, even so I do, Arise, let us go hence. These were some great prayers Jesus prayed for everyone.

John 14:1-31

As I bring my book to a close, I want to share with you one of my most loved parts of the Bible that I treasure so dearly. It's a prayer Jesus prayed, and it's in the gospel of John 17:

These words spoke Jesus and lifted up his eyes to heaven and said, Father, the hour is come; glorify thy Son, that thy Son may glorify thee; As you have given him power over all flesh, that he should give eternal life to as many as you have given him, And this is life eternal, that they might know you, the only true God, and Jesus Christ whom you have sent. I have glorified you on the earth; I have finished the work which you gave me to do. And now O Father, glorify thou me with thine own self with the glory which I had with you before the world was. I have manifested thy name unto the men which you gave me out of the world: thine they were, and you gave them to me: and they have kept thy word. Now they have known that all things whatsoever thou hast given me are of thee. For I have given unto them the words which you gave me; and have received them, and have known surely that I came out from thee, and they have believed that you did send me. I pray for them; I pray not for the world, but for them which you have given me; they are thine, And all mine is thine and thine are mine; and I am glorified in them. And now I am no more in the world, but these are in the world, and I come to thee. Holy Father, keep through thine own name those whom you have given me, that they may be one as we are. While I was with them in the world, I kept them in thy name; those that you gave me I have kept, and none of them is lost, but the son of perdition, that the scripture might be fulfilled. And now come I to thee; and these things I speak in the world, that they might have my joy fulfilled in themselves. I have given them thy word; and the world has hated them, because they are not of the world, even as I am not of the world. I pray not that you should take them out of the world, but that you should keep them from the evil. They are not of the world, even as I am not of the world. Sanctify them through thy truth: thy word is truth. As you have sent me into the world, even so have I also sent them into the world. And for their sakes I sanctify myself, that they also might be sanctified through the truth. Neither pray I for these alone, but for them also which shall believe on me through their word. That they all may be one; as thou Father art in me, and I in them, that they also may be one in us: that the world may believe that you have sent me. And the glory which you gave me I have given them; that they may be one, even as we are one. I in them, and thou in me; that they may be made perfect in one; and that the world may know that you have sent me, and have loved them as you have loved me. Father, I will that they also, whom you have given me, be with me where I am; that they may behold my glory which you have given me before the foundation of the world. O righteous Father, the world has not known thee; but I have known thee, and these have known that you have sent me. And I have declared unto them thy name, and will declare it, that the love wherewith you have loved me may be in them, and I in them.

John 17:1-26

Every time I read this prayer Jesus prayed, it encourages me and reminds me of the great love God has for us.

CHAPTER 39

Finally; I would like to share with you a little from my first book, a Christian fiction novel, *The Recurring Dream:*

This was a word of prophesy to the congregation during a church service. That God is all for you and not against you, nothing can compare to knowing that God loves you and his thoughts towards you are good and not of evil. He wants you to have a Hope and a future.

God bless you,
Billy Arcand.

My Word is true, and I do accomplish what I say in my Word. It's sad to see people miss my blessings because of their disobedience. Please be assured though in knowing that the children who they killed, are with me in Heaven. Your enemy is trying to tear millions more away, but my Glory will not only be over America, but upon the whole world. Out of your belly shall flow rivers of living water. I love you, and in just a little while, my Glory shall be with you so mightily that nothing will hold you back, for I am with you. I want you to know that I inhabit your praises and rejoice over you with singing. I love you so much that I even store your tears in precious viols in Heaven. I myself will wipe away all your tears. There will be no more tears or crying in Heaven, for the former things will pass away. Your life can be one of joy unspeakable and full of glory here and now, but eternity will hold a joy you have never known. Hold on my child, Hold on. I know it seems like a long time to you, but soon you will see my Glory. I knew you before you were born. Keep on keeping on. Don't be discouraged, for in due season, you will see the Salvation of the Lord, and realize I never left you. My Word will not fail. It will be fulfilled. My waters will flow, and my disciples shall be as the stars of Heaven. Multitudes upon multitudes will know my Word and follow hard after me. I will raise up my people from all walks of life, poor, rich, black, white, young, and old will be a part of my plan. They will come from the north, south, east, and west. One word of wisdom I must give you: It's up to you, for you are my hands and feet on the earth. Experience the Blessings of obedience by taking part in stopping abortions, and preach my Word. Be diligent and Pray. Get involved, Amen.

Finally, to all the people of God, I pray you will be enlightened and that you have a deeper revelation of God's purpose and plan for your life. Please know that I wrote this book not to put down or criticize anyone. I wrote this book because I wanted you to know the same God that I know through many years; over 50 years of exploring through the Bible, God's Word.

I hope you enjoyed reading my book. If you feel you have a better understanding of God and His love for you. You may use my book in a Bible study if you choose. Maybe you have a friend or family member struggling with something they might not know about God. Share my book with him or her. When you know the truth, the truth shall set you free.

CPSIA information can be obtained
at www.ICGtesting.com
Printed in the USA
LVHW011113130421
684341LV00020B/666